THE LIGHTS IN
THE TUNNEL

THE LIGHTS IN THE TUNNEL

AUTOMATION, ACCELERATING TECHNOLOGY AND THE ECONOMY OF THE FUTURE

Martin Ford

Acculant™
PUBLISHING

Copyright © 2009 by Martin R. Ford

All Rights Reserved,
including the right of reproduction
in whole or in part in any form.

Published in the United States by Acculant™ Publishing.

Library of Congress Cataloging-in-Publication Data
Ford, Martin R.
The Lights in the Tunnel: Automation, Accelerating Technology and
the Economy of the Future / Martin Ford
p. cm.
Includes bibliographical references
ISBN-10 1-4486-5981-7
ISBN-13 978-1-4486-5981-4
1. Economics—Future Trends 2. Economics—Impact of Advanced
Technology on 3. Artificial Intelligence and Robotics 4. Computer
Technology and Civilization 5. Technological Unemployment I. Title

This book is available for purchase in paper and electronic formats at:

www.TheLightsintheTunnel.com

Printed in the United States of America.

CONTENTS

Contents

INTRODUCTION

Like most people, I have been giving a lot of thought to the economic situation as the most serious crisis since the Great Depression has continued to unfold. Since I develop software and run a high tech business, I also spend a great deal of time thinking about computer technology, and so I began to focus on how economics and technology intertwine. The current crisis has been perceived as primarily financial in origin, but is it possible that ever advancing technology is an unseen force that has contributed significantly to the severity of the downturn? More importantly, what economic impact will technological acceleration have as we anticipate recovery from the current crisis—and in the years and decades ahead? What will the economy of the future look like?

Among people who work in the field of computer technology, it is fairly routine to speculate about the likelihood that computers will someday approach, or possibly even exceed, human beings in general capability and intelligence. Speaking at an industry conference in 2007, Google co-founder Larry Page said, "We have some people at Google [who] are really trying to build artificial intelligence and to do it on a large scale. It's not as far off as people think."[1] Ray Kurzweil, a well-known inventor, author and futurist, states quite categorically that he expects computers to become at least as intelligent as humans by the year 2029.[2] While other experts are far more conservative about the prospect for machines that can achieve genuine intelligence, there can be little doubt that computers and robots are going to become dramatically more capable and flexible in the coming years and decades.

What is the likely economic impact of machines or computers that begin to catch up with—and maybe even surpass—the average person's capability to do a typical job? Clearly, the employment market would be one of the first areas to feel that influence. Put yourself in the position of a business owner and think of all the problems that are associated with human employees: vacation, safety rules, sick time, payroll taxes, poor performance…maternity leave. If an affordable machine can do nearly any routine job as well as a human worker, then what business manager in his or her right mind would hire a worker?

Even if computers never become truly intelligent, surely machines are likely to become far more capable in terms of their ability to perform a relatively narrow range of tasks. The reality is that a substantial fraction of the routine, specialized jobs held by average people—including many people with college degrees—simply do not really require the full intellectual breadth of a human being. This is the reason that a lot of jobs are boring. If computers can already beat the best chess players in the world, isn't it likely that they will also soon be able to perform many routine jobs? In fact, I think there are good reasons to expect that machines may begin to approach this more specialized level of "intelligence" within a decade or two.

Since many of the people who work in fields like artificial intelligence and robotics are talking about the future prospects for these technologies on a fairly regular basis, I assumed that a similar discussion must be going on among economists. Surely, the economists are thinking ahead. If machines suddenly get smarter and start doing many of our jobs, then the economists will have a plan in place. At least they will have thought about it; they'll have some good suggestions. Right?

Well, no. It turns out that while technologists are actively thinking about, and writing books about, intelligent machines, the idea that technology will ever truly replace a large fraction of the human workforce and lead to permanent, structural unemployment is, for the majority of economists, almost *unthinkable*. For mainstream economists, at least in the long run, technological advancement always leads to more prosperity and more jobs. This is seen almost as an economic *law*. Anyone who challenges this "law of economics" is called a "neo-Luddite." This is not a compliment. (We'll talk about Luddites and the associated "Luddite fallacy" in some detail in Chapter 2 of this book.)

While most economists dismiss the question completely, the technical people seem to be entirely caught up in the excitement of the technology itself and what it might potentially promise. There is some discussion of the fact that artificial intelligence might have serious impacts on society, but much of this is focused on the threat of truly advanced or even sentient machines in some way "taking over." There is little attention given to the more mundane and immediate threats to the job market and the overall economy. Perhaps the technologists just assume that once the technology comes along, the economic issues will somehow work themselves out.

Now that is an unsupportable assumption. It would probably be reasonable to assume that technical problems will sort themselves out. Technology usually seems to find a way. But economic policy and political issues? Think back to 1993. Bill Clinton had just been elected and had promised to reform the health care system. As we all know, that effort failed. The major issues back in 1993 were very similar to what we continue to face in 2009. As this is being written, Congress is once again taking up the issue of comprehensive health care reform. It has taken a full 16 years to get to this point, and still the outcome is by no means certain.

But what happened with technology? In 1993, hardly anyone had heard of the Internet: it was something that people in government and at universities used primarily for work-related email. Some people had primitive cell phones. Microsoft had just introduced Windows 3.1, which for the first time brought a usable graphical interface to IBM PC-compatible computers. The evidence is pretty clear: a race between technology and our ability to reform our political and economic systems is really no race at all. So if we can foresee that technology is likely to have a highly disruptive impact on our economy in the coming years and decades, then we really need to start thinking about that well in advance.

The disintegration of the Soviet Union in 1991 demonstrated quite conclusively that there is no good alternative to the free market system. Other economic systems simply cannot compete. In fact, it's probably reasonable to say that the free market economy is one of mankind's greatest inventions—ranking right up there with the wheel. The wealth and progress that we enjoy in the industrialized world would not have come into being without the underlying logic of capitalism. Historically, technology and the market economy have worked together to make us all more wealthy. Will this always be true? Is it simply a matter of leaving the system we have in place?

The reality is that the free market economy, as we understand it today, simply cannot work without a viable labor market. Jobs are the primary mechanism through which income—and, therefore, purchasing power—is distributed to the people who consume everything the economy produces. If at some point, machines are likely to permanently take over a great deal of the work now performed by human beings, then that will be a threat to the very foundation of our economic system. This is not something that will just work itself out. This is something that we need to begin thinking about—and that is the primary subject of this book.

Once you identify and begin to think about the economic ramifications of advancing technology, it becomes clear that these trends are already well established and may even underlie the current crisis to a significant extent. If you make some very logical, and even conservative, assumptions about where technology is likely to lead in the coming years, much of the conventional wisdom about what the future will look like becomes unsupportable. In particular, important trends such as globalization simply may not play out in the way we have been led to expect. If we do not recognize these issues and adapt to the changes they imply, it will be very difficult—perhaps impossible—to achieve a sustainable recovery that will lead to long-term prosperity in the years and decades to come.

As we will see, technology is not just advancing gradually: it is accelerating. As a result, the impact may come long before we expect it—and long before we are ready. And yet, this issue is simply not on the radar. If after reading this book, you are concerned about the issues raised here, then I hope you will consider speaking out. Perhaps if enough people start to discuss these issues, even the economists will take notice.

Chapter 1

THE TUNNEL

What if technology progresses to the point where a substantial fraction of the jobs now performed by people are instead performed autonomously by machines or computers? Is that likely, or even possible? And if it is, what are the implications for our economy?

In this book, we are going to explore what increasing technological advancement, and in particular job automation, could mean to the economies of developed countries like the United States and also to the world economy as a whole. To do this, we are going to start by creating an imaginary simulation (or mental video game) that should provide some very useful insight into what we can expect in the future.

As we all know, in recent years the practice of offshoring, or outsourcing jobs to countries like India where wages are lower, has attracted a great deal of controversy. Many people in a variety of jobs and professions in the U.S. and other developed countries are now very concerned that their jobs might eventually be moved overseas.

While offshoring seems to get most of the attention at the moment, we also know that automation—the complete replacement of human jobs by machines—continues to go on in a variety of industries.

There are certain conventional views that most of us accept regarding these practices. For example, we are told that although automation and offshoring may result in significant job losses in certain industries, types of jobs, or geographic regions, this is part of the normal functioning of the free market economy. As jobs are eliminated in one area, economic growth and innovation create new opportunities. As a result, new products and services are developed, new businesses arise and new jobs are created.

We also know that practices like the offshoring of jobs and the relocation of manufacturing to low wage countries like China are creating new opportunities for workers in those countries. As a result, a massive new middle class is being created. As those newly wealthy people enter the world market, they create dramatic new worldwide demand for consumer products and services. Businesses in countries throughout the world will thus enjoy access to new markets, and as a result, new jobs will be created everywhere. In short, the general belief is that the trends toward globalization and automation may create temporary displacements and pockets of unemployment, but ultimately, technological progress creates new jobs and makes all of us more wealthy.

In this chapter, we are going to start off by creating a mental simulation that *rejects* these conventional wisdoms. We are instead going to make the following assumption:

At some point in the future—it might be many years or decades from now—machines will be able to do the jobs of a large percentage of the "average" people in our population, and these people will <u>not</u> be able to find new jobs.

Many people might disagree with this assumption; they may feel strongly that in our economy, new jobs will *always* be created. Let's leave that aside for the moment; we'll discuss it in great detail in the next chapter. For now, let's just go ahead and use this assumption. After all, it's only a simulation.

Who are these "average" people whose jobs we are going to simulate away? We simply mean the bulk of the working people in our population. Let's say at least 50 to 60 percent of the employed population. These are just typical people doing typical jobs. In the United States, about 28 percent[3] of the adult population has a college degree. So many of these average people may have gone to college or even graduate school, but most have not. They are the people who drive trucks, fix cars, and work in department stores, supermarkets and all types of offices and factories. They probably are not neurosurgeons, and they most likely do not have a PhD from MIT. They work on the loading dock, sell insurance or real estate or laptop computers, work in customer service, or accounting, in a variety of small businesses or at the post office. They are what we all think of as regular people.

So our assumption is going to be that, at some point down the line, machines or computers will take over a great many of these people's jobs. Not all of them, but a lot. Maybe 40 percent. Maybe half. The exact number doesn't really matter.

We are also assuming that, although these people might try very hard, they simply *will not* be able to find another job. Perhaps another job is created somewhere else in the economy, but maybe that job requires very advanced or specific education, skills or training, so that we can't have any reasonable expectation that this "average" person can fill that job. Or then again, maybe *no* new job is created. Maybe the new job just gets automated right away.

Before we get started with our simulation, let's look at the idea of the world mass market.

The Mass Market

Each of us, if we are lucky enough to live in one of the advanced nations of the world, enjoys access to an immense variety of products and services. As you walk through one of the large consumer electronics retail stores, you are confronted with a seemingly limitless number of different products in a variety of price ranges. Similarly if you enter a large bookstore, you'll be presented with literally thousands of different books, music CDs and movie DVDs.

This tremendous selection of products, and also services, which we now take for granted, is unprecedented in human history. Never before has such a variety been available—and certainly not to the "typical" people who comprise the majority of the population. All these products owe their existence to the mass market. In today's world, a business that sells mp3 players, cell phones, laptop computers, personal financial services, or automobiles sees a potential market comprised of tens or, in some cases, even hundreds of millions of potential buyers. It is this seemingly limitless ocean of good customer prospects that makes very high volume production and marketing possible.

When a business creates products or services at high volume, it realizes economies of scale, and that, of course, results in lower prices. In addition, however, high volume production also makes it possible for the business to adopt statistical quality control techniques and to improve overall consistency and precision in the production process. The result is not just cheaper products—but better and more reliable products.

Because of the mass market, we enjoy a seemingly infinite variety of choices, and we also have come to expect products and services of consistently high quality. For most of us, the benefits of the mass market have had such a deep impact, that in a very real sense, they have become integrated into our culture and now govern the expectations that we have for the quality of our daily lives.

Visualizing the Mass Market

So that we can better understand how the mass market works, let's now create our mental simulation or "video game" of the market. Once we can visualize a working simulation, we can return to our original question about the impact of automation and see what might happen.

Before we start, I should mention that in order to keep things simple, we are thinking in terms of a single worldwide mass market. In fact, we know that different regions and countries actually have distinct but highly connected markets. The markets are currently kept separate by things like geographic distance, language barriers, incompatibilities (many U.S. cell phones won't work elsewhere for example), and cultural differences. However, we know that continuing forces such as globalization and the Internet have caused the markets to become much more closely linked than in the past. For this reason, we can safely use a simple one-market model for our simulation.

* * * * *

To visualize the mass market, think of a vast tunnel. The tunnel is dark, but streaming though the tunnel are countless points of white light. The lights float along at a somewhat leisurely pace like tiny moving stars. Each light represents a single person (or consumer) who participates in the world mass market.

The number of lights seems limitless, but in fact they represent only a small fraction of the world's population. The lights include the people of the United States, Canada, Western Europe, Japan, Australia, New Zealand, and other developed nations. Also among the lights are wealthy people from throughout the world and the fast-growing middle classes in developing countries like China, India, Russia and Brazil. All told, there are perhaps somewhere around a billion lights in the tunnel.

The brightness of each light represents the purchasing power (or discretionary income) of each person. In order to enter the tunnel and participate in the mass market, a person must meet a certain threshold of purchasing power.

If we could go outside the tunnel, we would find over five billion barely perceptible lights. These dimly lit lights represent the world's poor: the approximately 80 percent of the population that lives on less than ten dollars per day.[4] These lights are, of course, eager to enter the tunnel. However, they are prevented from entering until they can achieve the necessary threshold of brightness. Nonetheless, at the entrance to the tunnel, we can see that a continuous stream of lights suddenly begin to shine more brightly and are thus able to enter the mass market. As we have said, these are the growing middle classes of China, India and other nations. The number of lights in the tunnel is constantly growing.

As we watch the lights float past, we notice that the vast majority shine with a medium range of brightness. These are the average (or typical) people who make up the middle class populations of the world.

Looking closely, we can see that there are also a significant number of much dimmer lights. These are the marginal participants in the mass market—people who just meet the threshold for remaining in the tunnel. These people either hold the very lowest paying jobs, or in many cases, they subsist on government transfer payments, such as welfare or unemployment insurance. Many of the dim lights stay that way only for a short time. They may be unemployed for a while but then find a new job and quickly begin to shine more brightly. Many others, however, are caught in the cycle of poverty and remain dim indefinitely.

These people must constantly fight to stay above the threshold of brightness that keeps them in the tunnel. Some will fail. Even in the United States, there are people, such as the homeless, who have been cast out from the tunnel.

Finally, we see that there are a fewer number of lights which shine much more brightly than the rest. These are wealthy people. Many of these people have advanced educations or specialized skills and, as a result, earn a high income. We can see that among these bright lights there is also a range of brightness. We notice that the brighter the lights, the fewer they are in number. At the extreme, we can very occasionally see an intensely bright light, shining like a miniature sun. These are the truly rich people of the world: people who through inheritance or entrepreneurship or other means have acquired vast amounts of wealth.

Still, as we watch the scene inside the tunnel, it is the *overwhelming number of the average lights* that truly captivates us. We can feel instinctively that it is these average lights that collectively represent the true power of the mass market.

Now let's change our perspective so that we are inside the tunnel with the lights. Looking around us, we see that the walls of the tunnel are alive with a continuous mosaic of color and motion. The tunnel walls are tiled with thousands upon thousands of flat panel displays. Each display runs a continuous advertisement for a product or service that is offered for sale in the mass market. These panels vary greatly in size and arrangement.

Some panels are huge and are arranged in clusters, each advertising a specific product. These are the large corporations that have become household names. Although the large companies stand out, we can see that huge areas of the tunnel walls are covered in a patchwork of many thousands of much smaller panels. These are the products and services offered by small businesses that also cater to the mass market.[1]

As we continue to watch the lights, we can now see that they are attracted to the various panels. We watch as thousands of lights steam toward a large automaker's panels, softly make contact and then bounce back toward the center of the tunnel. As the lights touch the panel, we notice that they dim slightly while the panel itself pulses with new energy. New cars have been purchased, and a transfer of wealth has taken place.

We know that a natural cycle exists within the tunnel. Almost instantly, we can see that many thousands of lights scattered randomly throughout the tunnel shine a little more brightly. These are the employees of the automaker being refreshed with new light. Another transfer of wealth has taken place. The autoworkers in turn make purchases from other business, small and large, and the light continues to parade through the tunnel.

We also know that behind the walls of the tunnel there are more businesses and interconnections that we

---

[1] We can also imagine that small, locally oriented businesses (such as restaurants) are included in our tunnel. While these businesses obviously don't cater directly to the global mass market, they are nonetheless integrated into the activity that occurs in the tunnel, and they are heavily impacted by the overall health and vitality of the mass market.

can't see. A large steel company receives payment from the automobile manufacturer and, in turn, its employees shine with new light.

If we could watch the action in the tunnel over a long period of time, we would find that the tunnel is not at all a static place. We would notice that some of the panels on the walls gradually grow dimmer and attract fewer lights. In some cases, they may reverse their decline and become strong again. But in many other cases, they weaken and grow dark.

Even as this happens, however, elsewhere on the tunnel walls, we see that new panels are appearing and growing stronger. A few seem to grow rapidly in size before our eyes. This is the process of *creative destruction*. In the mass market, the collective purchasing decisions of the lights determine which businesses succeed and thrive, and which ones ultimately decline and fail. This is a natural and cyclical process. When an inefficient business fails, its capital, resources and employees will eventually be transferred to a new, stronger business. As a panel on the tunnel wall goes dark, the lights that represent that company's workers will also grow dim. But over time, they will find new jobs and their light will be restored.

We now have a pretty clear picture of how the mass market works. We see the lights streaming toward and contacting various panels, and then, elsewhere in the tunnel, other lights brightening as wealth is cycled between consumers, businesses and workers within the tunnel. Over time, we see panels die and other new panels spring up, as old businesses that can no longer compete in the market are replaced with new, more competitive start-ups, often in completely new and different industries.

We can also feel that, in general, the total amount of light in the tunnel is increasing. This is partly due to the new lights constantly streaming into the tunnel, but we also have the sense that as the light is cycled throughout the tunnel, its intensity seems to very gradually increase of its own volition—as though the very process of moving the light around naturally makes it grow over time.

This then is the mass market: a natural cycle of increasing light and wealth governed by the logic of the marketplace. It is the primary engine of our free market economy.

Automation Comes to the Tunnel

Now that we have a working simulation of the mass market, let's go ahead and perform our experiment with job automation. To keep things simple, let's first focus on the issue of jobs being taken over completely by machines or computers and leave the question of offshoring for later.

* * * * *

Now we are back in our tunnel. Very gradually, we begin to eliminate the jobs held by many of the average lights. As this happens, the impacted lights grow dimmer and in many cases disappear completely.

The automation process affects jobs throughout the world. In developed countries, the people who lose their jobs will usually continue to receive income, at least for a time, from government programs such as unemployment insurance. However, as we have seen, these programs generally produce only very dim lights. In third world countries with little or no safety net, these unlucky people will likely be cast out from the tunnel, and their light will disappear entirely.

The impact of automation is still very difficult to discern among the multitude of lights in the tunnel. We notice, however, that some of the brightest lights in the tunnel are beginning to shine with even more intensity. As jobs are eliminated, many of the businesses in the tunnel become more profitable. Some of this wealth is then transferred to the owners and top executives of the businesses. As this process continues, we see the brighter lights continue to slowly gain strength as more of the average lights gradually dim or flicker out. The distribution of income is becoming more concentrated in the tunnel.

Now, finally, we begin to see a real difference in the tunnel. It becomes obvious that there are fewer lights and that the number is continuing to diminish. Just as this realization strikes us, we immediately feel that there is a new sense of urgency pervading the panels that line the walls of the tunnel. The panels begin to dance with more and more desperate motion and color as they attempt to attract the dwindling number of lights.

The businesses on the walls of the tunnel are now suddenly seeing significantly slower demand for their products and services. This is happening even though many of the brightest lights in the tunnel have continued to gain in strength.

Imagine that your job is to sell as many $50 cell phones as you can in one hour. You are offered two doors: Behind door #1 sit Bill Gates and Warren Buffet, the two richest people in America. Behind door #2 are a thousand average people. You may well be tempted to choose the first door just so you'll get to meet Bill and Warren, but in terms of getting your job done, you would probably agree that door #2 is clearly the best choice. This is because the demand for the mass market products that drive our economy depend much more on the *number* of potential customers than on the wealth of any particular customer. You are not going to be able to sell 40 cell phones to one person, no matter how wealthy they are.

We can now sense that many of the businesses in the tunnel are clearly in trouble. Even though they are continuing to save money as automation slowly eliminates some of their remaining workers, this is not enough to make up for the reduction in sales they are experiencing. Many of these companies are now at the point where they must take action to survive.

A great deal of each company's resources is invested in factories, machines and equipment and offices. These things, which an economist might refer to as capital, are very hard to quickly get rid of. For example, if you just bought a lot of new automated machines for your factory, then you are stuck with them. You can't just return them and get your money back if demand for your products suddenly starts to fall. For this reason, a business which sees rapidly falling demand usually has only one choice in order to survive: cut more jobs. We see this, of course, as part of the normal business cycle. Businesses routinely lay off workers in bad times and then rehire in good times.

In the tunnel, we now see that the businesses are beginning to cut more and more jobs. They are becoming more desperate and, in many cases, they must eliminate even key employees that they formerly felt were crucial to their operations. As this happens, we begin to see some of the brighter lights in the tunnel rapidly begin to dim.

The continuing decrease in demand falls especially heavily on the manufacturing businesses located in developing nations like China. These businesses rely on producing very high volume products, which they export to first world nations. They are now severely cutting jobs and the flow of new middle class people into the tunnel has all but stopped.

As a result of the job cuts, the lights are becoming even more sparse in the tunnel. Many of the businesses are now failing and whole regions of the tunnel walls are growing dark. Now we see that many of the very brightest lights in the tunnel finally feel the impact and also begin to lose their light. The owners of the businesses in the tunnel are seeing much of their wealth gradually drain away.

The tunnel has become a far darker and more stagnant place. We sense clearly that the hopes of even the remaining brighter lights are gradually evaporating into the new emptiness of the tunnel.

A Reality Check

Clearly, our simulation did not turn out well. Perhaps our initial assumption about jobs being automated was wrong. But, again, let's leave that for the next chapter. In the meantime, we might wonder if we have made a mistake somewhere in the simulation. Let's see if we can perform some type of "reality check" on our result. Perhaps we can look to history to see if there is anything in the past that might support what we saw happen in our simulation.

Let's leave our tunnel and travel back in time to the year 1860. In the southern part of the United States, we know we will find the greatest injustice ever perpetrated in the history of our nation. Here, long before the new light of advanced technology first began to shine, men had discovered a far more primitive and perverse form of job automation.

The injustice and moral outrage associated with slavery rightly attracts nearly all of our attention. For this reason, most of us don't have occasion to think about the overall *economic* impact of slavery. At the time Abraham Lincoln was elected president, we know that while the Northern population's moral objection to slavery was a primary divisive issue, there were also significant differences and debate about issues relating to the differing economic systems of the North and the South.

The Northern economy was built on free labor and entrepreneurship and tended to spread opportunity more equally throughout the population. In contrast, the Southern states relied on slave labor, and wealth was primarily concentrated in the hands of white plantation owners who owned many slaves. One result of this system was that it was very hard for poorer whites to advance their situation because relatively few free labor opportunities were available.

Documented observations illustrate the impact of slavery on the Southern economy. In her book *Team of Rivals: The Political Genius of Abraham Lincoln*, Doris Kearns Goodwin describes a journey that William Seward, who would years later become Lincoln's Secretary of State, took in 1835. Seward traveled with his family from his home in New York State to the slave state of Virginia.[5] As the Sewards cross into Virginia they leave behind the bustling towns and cities to which they had become accustomed. Instead, they travel a rough, deserted road with few homes, businesses or taverns. Dilapidated shacks dot the landscape, and the land itself seems to have been assaulted by poverty. During his journey, Seward observed: "How deeply the curse of slavery is set upon this venerated and storied region of the old dominion. Of all the countries I have seen France only whose energies have for forty years been expended in war and whose population has been more decimated by the sword is as much decayed as Virginia."[6]

It seems clear that there are some definite parallels between what we saw in our simulation and the slave economy in the South. We noticed that in our tunnel, the brightest lights initially became even brighter as the average lights began to dim and flicker out. This fits well with the fact that most wealth in the South was concentrated in the hands of rich plantation owners, while the majority of the population was trapped in poverty.

There is one important discrepancy, however. In our simulation, the situation continued to deteriorate until even the brightest lights eventually began to lose their strength. In contrast, slavery in the Southern states lasted for over two hundred years. The plantation owners were able to hold onto their wealth at least until the start of the Civil War in 1861. If our simulation seems to indicate that a slave (or automation-based) economy is destined to undergo continuing decline, how is it that the slave states were able to maintain stability for so long?

The answer lies in the fact that the South was primarily an *export* economy. The large plantations produced raw cotton which was then shipped to Europe and to the Northern states where it was manufactured into textiles and clothing. It was this constant wealth flowing in from the outside that was able to maintain the economy over time.

Our simulation, of course, was of the entire world mass market, so there was obviously no export market available. In the simulation, we found that across-the-board automation of jobs eventually reduced demand for products and services as the number of lights in the tunnel decreased. You can imagine that, if the South had been completely isolated economically with no outside trade allowed, it would likely have followed a path of decline similar to the one we saw in the simulation.

In fact, one of President Lincoln's first acts after the Southern states seceded from the Union was to implement a complete blockade of the South. The blockade became increasingly effective as the years progressed—ultimately achieving a 95 percent reduction in Southern cotton exports—and was certainly an important factor in the outcome of the war. By the time the war ended in 1865, the Southern economy was in complete ruin. One can speculate that if the blockade could have been maintained without an actual shooting war taking place, the economic impact alone might have in time led to the end of slavery.[1]

Summarizing

Both our tunnel simulation and our examination of the Southern slave economy seem to support the idea that once full automation penetrates the job market to a substantial degree, an economy driven by mass-market production must ultimately go into decline. The reason for this is simply that, when we consider the market as a whole, the people who rely on jobs for their income are the *same individuals* who buy the products produced.

Another way of expressing this is to say that although machines may take over people's jobs, the machines—unless we are really going to jump into the stuff of science

---

[1] Is it really reasonable to draw a comparison between the economic effects of slavery and advanced machine automation? I would argue that the comparison almost certainly *underestimates* the economic impact of autonomous machines. Because of its inhumanity, slavery carries with it obvious costs. These include both the direct costs of enslaving unwilling human beings as well as lost productivity. The owners of machines would, of course, see none of these costs. In addition, machines, which can operate essentially continuously, obviously have the potential to be far more productive than even a willing human worker could be.

fiction—do not participate in the market as consumers. Recall from our example of selling cell phones to the two billionaires or to a thousand regular people, that making a few people richer *will not* make up for losing a large number of potential customers. That may work for yachts and Ferraris but not for the mass produced products and services that are the backbone of our economy.

At the very beginning of the automation process this effect was not at all clear. The first businesses to automate saw a significant reduction in their costs as they cut workers, while the impact on the demand for their products was negligible—or in fact, demand may have actually increased for a time, as they were able to lower their prices. As a result, their profits, and therefore the wealth of their top employees and shareholders increased. These were the brighter lights in the tunnel that initially became stronger.

However, as *nearly all businesses* in the tunnel continued to automate jobs, at some point the decrease in the number of potential customers began to outweigh the advantages gained from automation. Once this happened, businesses were forced to cut even more jobs, which eliminated even more consumers from the market and caused demand to fall still further. From this point on, the economy entered a continuing downward spiral.

Not a very happy ending. However, we still need to examine our initial assumption. Is it really possible that, at some point in the future, machines or computers could take over the jobs performed by a large percentage of average workers *without* new jobs within the capability of these people being created? Could that really happen?

We'll look at that question in the next chapter. We'll also look at something called the *Luddite fallacy*—which is an established line of economic reasoning that strongly contradicts the result we saw in our simulation.

Chapter 2

ACCELERATION

Let's now turn to the question of whether or not the assumption we made about jobs being automated in the future is a reasonable one. It might be helpful to start by turning that assumption inside out and looking at its converse. If you believe the assumption we made is incorrect, then you must believe that:

Technology will <u>never</u> advance to the point where the bulk of jobs performed by typical people will be automated. The economy will always create jobs that are within the capabilities of the vast majority of the human population.

When you look at things this way, you might see some cause for concern. The real problem, of course, is that one offending word: "never." Never is a very long time: it is three hundred or a even a thousand years. Never is, well, forever.

To make things more reasonable, let's lower the standard somewhat. Let's think in terms of our own lifetimes or the lives of our children. That should make the issue much more approachable and personal. After all, surely none of us would want something dramatically negative to happen during the lives of our own children, even if we weren't around to see it.

With that standard in mind, let's just assume a reasonable average lifespan of 80 years for a baby born today. That gives us the year 2089 as a cutoff date. So the assumption that we want to test now becomes:

Technology will not advance to the point where the bulk of jobs performed by typical people will be automated before the year 2089. Prior to that year, the economy will always create jobs that are within the capabilities of the vast majority of the human population.

Can we bank on that?

The Rich Get Richer

Nearly all of us sense that our world is changing rapidly and that perhaps things seem to be speeding up. We've become accustomed especially to continuous improvement in technology. We notice that the laptop computer we buy today is dramatically faster and lighter and more feature-packed than the one we bought just a few years ago, and yet it costs less. Our new cell phone is smaller or lighter, but it does more.

As human beings, we are geared toward thinking in terms of constant motion or gradual change. We tend to analyze things in terms of straight lines. For the most part, this is how the physical world around us works.

We are, of course, familiar with the concept of acceleration. We experience it while driving or when an airplane takes off. But in the course of our daily lives, acceleration is—almost without exception—something that is of very short duration: something typically limited to seconds. Perhaps for this reason, it is not easy for us to really comprehend the idea of an acceleration that continues relentlessly for *decades*. It is difficult for us to really get our minds around the implications of this.

In 1965, Gordon E. Moore, the co-founder of Intel Corporation, observed that, as a result of constant innovation, the number of transistors on a silicon chip roughly doubled at a consistent pace. Moore speculated that the rate of growth would continue into the foreseeable future, and in the years since, his forecast has proven to be correct. Moore's observation initially related to the nuts and bolts of how chips are fabricated, but over time it has evolved into a broader rule of thumb that gives us a useful framework for thinking about how our ability to manipulate and process information increases over time. This rule of thumb has become known as *Moore's Law,*[*] and it can be expressed as follows:

As technology progresses, the computational capability of a computer will roughly double every two years.

Moore's Law is, of course, not a "law" at all—certainly not in the sense that physical rules like the ones postulated by Isaac Newton are laws. It is, however, an accurate observation and projection, and nearly everyone in the technology field accepts it. Moore's Law is an overall estimate. Different facets of technology, in fact, progress at different rates. Still, we can probably agree that it

---

[*] Some versions of Moore's Law use 18 months rather than 2 years as the doubling standard. I have chosen the more conservative number.

is our expanding ability to manipulate and communicate information that is the driving force behind the technical innovation we see all around us—and Moore's Law does an especially good job of capturing the rate of progress in that arena.

When something doubles at a regular pace, we say that it grows *geometrically*, or *exponentially*.* To illustrate the extraordinary acceleration that this implies, imagine starting with a penny and then doubling the amount you have every day for a month. You begin with one cent; on the second day you have two cents and then four cents on the third day, and so on.

The first chart on the next page shows the first fifteen days as our penny doubles. You can see that we start out very slowly and then begin to accelerate. On day fifteen, we have about $164—which is not bad at all since we started with only a penny!

In our next chart, we look at days 15-30. Now we've had to greatly expand the scale of our bar chart so we can accommodate some very big numbers toward the end. You can see that we start where we left off with $164, but now this amount is so tiny against our new scale that we don't even see a visible bar. We have to wait until day 22 before we see a hint of progress—but still that amount represents nearly 21 thousand dollars.

Things really start to fly from there. We pass the million-dollar mark at day 28 and end up on day 30 with over five million dollars. Not bad for a month's work. If we had

---

* These terms have slightly different technical meanings, but for our purposes they are interchangeable.

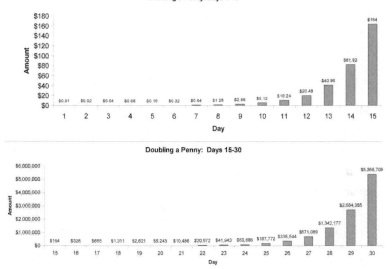

been lucky enough to choose a month with 31 days for our experiment, we would have nearly eleven million dollars to show for it. If we could continue the process for another thirty days, we would have an astonishing $5,764,607,523,034,235—or nearly six *quadrillion* dollars!

As you can see, a geometric or exponential progression is really the ultimate case of "the rich get richer." The more you have, the more you get, and it just keeps going. When we compare this with the more routine things we encounter in life, the contrast is astonishing. Consider economic growth, or perhaps the raise you might hope to get at work; in these things, we are happy to see a gain of a few percentage points. Can this be real? Is the computational capability of computers really expanding that fast?

To illustrate that this is indeed the case, let me use an example from my own experience. In 1981, I entered the University of Michigan as a freshman with plans to study computer engineering. Computer engineering was then a new discipline just introduced at Michigan and at a few other universities. Up until then, no one had been quite sure that computers were important enough to merit their own engineering field.

The University of Michigan had one of the most advanced computing centers in the country. The computer then in use was a state-of-the-art mainframe machine manufactured by the Amdahl Corporation. In my first computer programming course, we were assigned the task of writing and running a program using computer punch cards.[7]

To do this, you first went to the university bookstore and purchased a large box of blank punch cards. These were similar to, but a little longer than, standard index cards.

You then wrote your program using pencil and paper, and took your blank cards to a card punch machine at the computing center. You inserted a blank card in the machine and entered, or "keyed in," one line from your program. As you did this, the machine punched corresponding holes in the card. You repeated this for each line in your program. If you made a mistake, you had to throw the entire card away and start over. For a complex program, you might have to punch hundreds of cards.

Next, being very careful not to scramble or drop the stack of cards, you took them to a card reader machine. You fed the stack of cards into the machine and your program was entered into a long line of other programs waiting for the attention of the computer.

After a time, in some cases hours, you went to the print center and retrieved a paper printout of the results. Since it is virtually impossible to write a perfect program the first (or usually even second) time, you had to go through this process several times until you found and fixed the "bugs" in your program.

Obviously, the way we interact with computers has changed dramatically. I had to include a description of punch cards above for the benefit of younger readers who may not have seen these. What about the computer itself? The mainframe in use at Michigan then was an Amdahl 470/V8. This was a machine that probably occupied a significant portion of a room and cost somewhere in the neighborhood of two million dollars.

In order to compare the relative speeds of different computers, engineers have developed a measurement known as Millions of Instructions per Second, or MIPS. The MIPS rating of a computer is a bit like the horsepower rating of an engine. While each computer has a unique design, MIPS ratings give us a useful way to make rough comparisons.

If you imagine a software program running on a computer to be similar to someone playing a tune on a piano, then each computer instruction would correspond to one strike of the piano keys. The Amdahl mainframe at

Michigan had a rating of about seven MIPS.[8] So we can think of our piano player ripping along at *seven million* keystrokes per *second*. Obviously, that is a very fast piano player, and at the time, it was pretty good for a computer.

By the time I graduated from Michigan in 1985, things on campus had changed a great deal. The year before, Apple Computer had released the MacIntosh. The MacIntosh and its predecessor, the Apple Lisa, were the first commercially available personal computers to have a graphical interface and a mouse. The university had purchased dozens of these new computers, and students were now using them in their courses rather than the mainframe.

The original MacIntosh ran at about one MIPS.[9] In other words, it was about 1/7 as fast as the Amdahl mainframe. That seemed quite impressive. After all, the MacIntosh was this tiny thing that sat on your desk, while the Amdahl was a $2 million behemoth that required its own room.

Now let's look at how things progressed after I left college:

- By 1988, Intel's 386DX processor was running at 8.5 MIPS. This microprocessor was used in the first IBM PC's that could run early versions Microsoft Windows. Thus a desktop computer had now exceeded the speed of the Amdahl mainframe.
- By 1992, Intel's 486DX ran at about 54 MIPS or nearly eight times the speed of the old Amdahl mainframe. 486-based PC's were the first ma-

chines to really provide a useful platform for Microsoft Windows. Windows 3.1, also introduced in 1992, became an enormous commercial success for Microsoft.

- By 1999, the Intel Pentium III was rated at over 1,300 MIPS. Our piano player is now going at over a billion keystrokes per second. This is close to 200 times the speed of the old Amdahl.

- In 2008, an Intel Core 2 Extreme processor was rated at up to 59,000 MIPS. That's 59 billion piano keystrokes per second and over 8000 times the speed of our 1981-vintage $2 million Amdahl mainframe.

Obviously, things have progressed very impressively over the 24 or so years since I left college. What we are more interested in, however, is what will happen in the future.

We know from Moore's Law that computers are progressing at a geometric or a "rich get richer" rate where we double what we already have every two years. In the first chapter, I used an example where we thought about selling cell phones to Bill Gates and Warren Buffet. Let's drag Bill back into the story now and perform an experiment that might give us an idea of the level of future progress that we can expect.

Bill Gates left Harvard in 1975 to move to New Mexico and found Microsoft along with his partner Paul Allen. We can mark that date as being essentially the beginning of the personal computer industry. As Bill starts work in 1975, let's imagine that we slip our magic penny into his pocket. Bill's focused on other things, and he won't notice. We'll double the penny every two years and see how much Bill ends up with:

- The IBM PC, which uses Microsoft's MS-DOS software, is introduced in August 1981. This sets Microsoft on its path to success. Bill now has eight cents in his pocket.
- In March 1986, Microsoft goes public and its stock trades for the first time on the NASDAQ market. Bill has about 45 cents.[10]
- Windows 3.1 is introduced in 1992. For the first time, Microsoft began to offer some competition to Apple's MacIntosh. Bill now has about $3.60 in his pocket.
- Windows XP is introduced in 2001. Bill has about $82.

Let's zoom forward to 2009 and look in Bill's pocket: about $1,300. Obviously, it's a good thing Bill didn't pin his fortunes on our magic penny.

Consider everything that Bill Gates has accomplished over his career. He built Microsoft into the world's dominant software company and has now retired from full time work at the company to run his charitable foundation. After all that, in terms of our experiment to measure the geometric acceleration of technology, Bill has less than 1,500 dollars. However, we can also see that things have accelerated quite dramatically in the years between 2001 and 2009: in just eight years, Bill has gained over $1,200, compared with a gain of only $82 over the 26 years leading up to 2001.

We know from the charts we looked at earlier that Bill will eventually reach the million dollar mark. What can we say about the future?

- In 2015, Bill will have about $10,500 or eight times what he has in 2009.
- In 2021, Bill will have nearly $84,000 or 64 times the 2009 figure.
- In 2025, Bill will have almost $336,000 or about 258 times what he has in 2009.
- In 2031, Bill becomes a multi-millionaire. He will have 2.6 million dollars or 2000 times what he has in 2009.

Looking at these numbers, we can see that unless technical progress slows significantly, computers are going to get dramatically more powerful by 2031. That date is nearly 60 years before the cutoff date of 2089 that we set at the beginning of this chapter.

What would Bill have in 2089? 1.4 *quadrillion* dollars. This is over one *trillion* times the 2009 amount of $1,300!

These numbers should give you a sense of the incredible degree of technological acceleration we can expect over the coming years and decades. As futurist and inventor Ray Kurzweil writes, "Exponential [or geometric] growth is deceptive. It starts out almost imperceptibly and explodes with unexpected fury."[11]

How confident can we be that Moore's Law will continue to be sustainable in the coming years and decades?

Evidence suggests that it is likely to hold true for the fore-seeable future. At some point, current technologies will run into a fundamental limit as the transistors on computer chips are reduced in size until they approach the size of individual molecules or atoms. However, by that time, completely new technologies may be available. As this book was being written, Stanford University announced that scientists there had managed to encode the letters "S" and "U" within the interference patterns of quantum electron waves.[12] In other words, they were able to encode digital information within particles smaller than atoms. Advances such as this may well form the foundation of future information technologies in the area of quantum computing; this will take computer engineering into the realm of individual atoms and even subatomic particles.

Even if such breakthroughs don't arrive in time, and integrated circuit fabrication technology does eventually hit a physical limit, it seems very likely that the focus would simply shift from building faster individual processors to instead linking large numbers of inexpensive, commoditized processors together in parallel architectures. As we'll see in the next section, this is already happening to a significant degree, but if Moore's Law eventually runs out of steam, parallel processing may well become the primary focus for building more capable computers.

Even if the historical doubling pace of Moore's Law does someday prove to be unsustainable, there is no reason to believe that progress would halt or even become linear in nature. If the pace fell off so that doubling took four years (or even longer) rather than the current two years, that would still be an exponential progression that would bring about staggering future gains in computing power.[13]

Let's look at our original assumption again:

Technology will not advance to the point where the bulk of jobs performed by typical people will be automated before the year 2089. Prior to that year, the economy will always create jobs that are within the capabilities of the vast majority of the human population.

Does that seem reasonable now? But wait, there's more.

World Computational Capability

Back in 1975, it probably would have been quite easy to make a list of every computer in the world. Primarily, we would have found computers in government agencies, universities, and large corporations. A manufacturer like IBM could probably have given us a list showing where each computer was installed. In the preceding section, we talked about how the power and speed of computers has increased. If we took that geometric rate of increase and just applied it to the computers that existed in 1975, that would be an incredible expansion of computational power. But of course, we know that is not what happened.

The *number* of computers in the world has also increased at a fantastic rate. By some estimates, there are now over a billion personal computers in use. But it doesn't stop there. Computers in the form of embedded microprocessors are in our cell phones, mp3 players, car engines, appliances and in countless other places. Computers are everywhere.

In fact, we might speculate that both the power and the number of computers in the world are increasing at a geometric rate—or at least something close to it. That is clearly an incomprehensible increase in our total ability to manipulate information. If you consider the number of obsolete devices that have been thrown away since the PC was introduced, it's easy to see that the computing power in landfills today is many orders of magnitude beyond what existed in the world in 1975.

It seems impossible to imagine that such an incredible advance in our ability to compute and to process information could take place without it having a dramatic effect on general technology, economics and society in general. In fact, however, in many areas, change has not come as quickly as we perhaps might have expected.

Cars and airplanes now incorporate computers, but their overall design and operation is still, for the most part, what it was in 1975. NASA managed the Apollo missions and reached the moon without access to modern computing power. Even the space shuttle dates back to the introduction of the first PCs. Likewise, economists speak of something called the *productivity paradox*, which basically says that, at least until quite recently, the economy has not really shown the productivity gains you might expect given all the new computers that have been introduced into workplaces. The computer revolution seems, so far, to have largely turned its energy inward on itself, resulting in advances primarily in the information and communication areas.[']

I have the feeling that this staggering increase in our computational capability represents a pent up resource that is poised to burst out in new and unexpected ways. In the future, we can expect that many more traditional technologies, and in fact nearly every aspect of our lives, will change—perhaps very rapidly—in ways that we cannot foresee. As examples of what we might expect, let's look at two things that have already occurred: one that, at least so far, has been generally positive, and one that has been decidedly negative.

Grid and Cloud Computing

Grid computing is a rapidly growing field that focuses on leveraging not just the power of an individual computer, but also the large number of such computers now available. The idea is to tie many computers together using special software. A big computational problem can then be broken down into pieces and distributed across hundreds or even thousands of computers so that they can work on it simultaneously. Grid computing has the potential to bring an unprecedented level of computing power to bear on difficult problems in the areas of science and engineering.

One of the first and most notable applications of grid computing was in the Human Genome Project. This in-

---

['] Even much of biotechnology and genetics could be considered a type of information science because it is focused on cataloging and understanding the information in our DNA.

ternational project began in 1990 and was completed in 2003—two years ahead of schedule. The primary goal of the project was to sequence the entire human DNA molecule and to identify the 25,000 or so individual genes that comprise our genetic code. The process of decoding our DNA molecule and identifying each gene took a tremendous amount of computational resources, and grid computing played a significant role in this.

The genetic information obtained through the project is stored in databases and can be accessed by scientists and researchers via the Internet. The result is a fantastic source of knowledge that continues to be analyzed and which is certain to result in innumerable future advances in the fields of genetics, bio-engineering and medicine.

An especially interesting development in the field of grid computing is the idea that unused power on virtually any computer connected to the Internet can be integrated into a voluntary grid and deployed to solve big problems. Most computers, if left on, do nothing at all during large blocks of time, especially overnight. The idea to tie these computers together by having their owners donate unused computing power has sprung up in a number of places.

Stanford University's *folding@home* project is geared toward solving difficult problems in a specialized area of biochemistry known as "protein folding." Advances in this area have the potential to provide future solutions for cancer and for diseases such as Huntington's and Parkinson's. Another major player in this area is the *Berkeley Open Infrastructure for Network Computing* (*BOINC*). This special software, developed at the University of California, Berkeley, allows individuals to donate unused computer time to a variety of scientific projects, including SETI (The Search for Extraterrestrial Intelligence), climate prediction, cancer research, astrophysics, and many others. The software to participate in these programs can be downloaded from the web.'

In the future, we can anticipate that grid computing will become increasingly important. In addition, it is already evolving into what computer scientists refer to as "cloud computing." Essentially this will amount to a new architecture for leveraging the power of huge numbers of computers on an as needed basis: computational capability, together with specific applications, will be delivered as though it were a utility much like electric power. The trend toward grid and cloud computing offers a fantastic opportunity to deploy our incredible new computational capacity in areas that will undoubtedly bring positive advances in fields such as science and medicine. Our next example, however, is far less benign.

Meltdown

As nearly everyone knows, the "subprime" meltdown of 2007 was triggered when borrowers who did not have the best credit ratings began to default on their mortgages. We know that banks and mortgage companies made these loans in some cases because of honest miscalculation of the risks involved, and in other cases due to outright fraud. With expectations driven by the housing bubble, many lenders may have had the rather callous attitude that, even

---

' http://folding.stanford.edu and http://boinc.berkeley.edu

if the borrower could not handle the payments, the lender could minimize its exposure by foreclosing at a higher price.

What does that have to do with computers? Well, if that had been the entire story, then the subprime crisis would have still been serious, but it would have been contained within the U.S. It certainly would not have cascaded around the world and resulted in the global financial crisis that occurred in 2008.

For an explanation of why the crisis spread throughout the world, we have to start back in 1973. In that year, an academic paper was published which contained a mathematical formula called the *Black-Scholes Option Pricing Model*. This formula, for the first time, gave a way to calculate the approximate value of a stock option. Stock options, which represent the right to buy or sell a stock at a given price at some point in the future, had been traded on markets for some time, but no one knew how to calculate a precise value for them.

In the years that followed, and especially during the 1980s, a large number of people originally trained as physicists or mathematicians began to take much higher paying jobs on Wall Street. These guys (they were virtually all men) were referred to as "quants." The quants started working with the Black-Scholes formula and expanded it in new ways. They turned their formulas into computer programs and gradually began to create new types of derivatives based on stocks, bonds, indexes and many other securities or combinations of securities.[14]

As their computers got faster and faster, the quants were able to do more and more. They created new exotic derivatives based on strange combinations of things. They could magnify the reward (and risk) of a security. They could invert it, so you gained if the security fell in value. They could even try to capture the reward if an investment increased in value, but eliminate the risk if it went down— or at least they thought they could.

As housing prices continued to climb during the bubble, the subprime loans were packaged into mortgage-backed securities so that they could be traded like bonds. This had become standard practice for mortgages. However, in addition to that, new types of derivatives were created based on the packaged subprime loans. Most notable were "collateralized debt obligations" (or CDOs), which attempted to siphon off the lowest risk loans and repackage them into a security that could be marketed as a high quality investment. These new derivative securities were then sold to banks and financial institutions all over the world, with the understanding that they were very low risk investments.

When the subprime borrowers started defaulting, the value of the mortgage-backed securities plunged, and the derivatives did not work as expected. In many cases it was difficult or impossible to calculate their value. In addition, financial institutions had engaged in many other complex interrelationships based on exotic derivatives that were intended to help manage various risks. All this led to uncertainty that caused values to fall even more. The result was the downfall of Bear Stearns in March 2008, and the global crisis that followed.

The point of this, of course, is that it would have been impossible to create these weird derivatives without access to very powerful computers. If the subprime crisis had occurred in earlier years, it would certainly have been a far smaller event. It's worth noting that the meltdown started in 2007. As we are now in 2009, we know that the power of the computers on Wall Street desks has roughly doubled, even as the crisis has continued.

Exotic derivatives are, of course, not the only example of the dramatic impact of advancing computer technology on financial markets. On October 19, 1987, the stock market fell a staggering twenty percent in a single day. There was really no specific news event or other factor that might have explained the sudden drop. Many of the people involved in quantitative technologies on Wall Street at the time believe that the crash may have been precipitated by computer programs that traded autonomously in the hope of providing "portfolio insurance" for big investors.

As this is being written, articles are appearing in the press regarding the use of extremely fast Wall Street computers that allow transactions to be executed in fractions of a second. This practice, known as "flash trading," has quickly attracted the notice of the Securities and Exchange Commission and may result in new regulation.

As these examples show, we can expect that the rate of change and the volatility of nearly everything around us will be somehow amplified by the incredible increase in our ability to compute. We can also certainly expect that this dramatically expanded computational capacity will be focused increasingly on automating our jobs.

Later in this chapter, we'll look in more detail at several specific advancing technologies and how they might impact the job market and the economy in general. But first, let's now turn from machines to human beings. Is it possible that we can somehow "outrun" computers so we can all keep our jobs?

Diminishing Returns

In 1811, England was in the midst of the Industrial Revolution. That year, a group called the *Luddites* formed in Nottingham. The Luddites consisted of skilled textile workers who felt threatened by the introduction of mechanical looms that could be operated by low-paid, unskilled workers. They took their name from a man named Ned Lud who had reportedly destroyed one of these advanced looms. The Luddites' protests grew into outright riots and destruction of machines. The British government finally enacted harsh measures and the movement came to an end in 1812. Since then, the word "luddite" has, of course, evolved into a somewhat derogatory term for anyone opposed to technological progress or ill equipped to deal with new technologies.

Economists generally dismiss the idea that advancing technology will ever permanently displace humans and thereby continuously increase the unemployment rate. In other words, most mainstream economists fully accept our assumption at the beginning of this chapter. (Not the

"2089" version; the *never* one.) Those who have raised concerns in more recent times are dismissed as "neo-Luddites." Economists have also formulated something called the *Luddite fallacy* to help explain why the concerns of neo-Luddites are wrong. We'll look at this in a little more detail later.

Obviously, England is now a modern country, and the vast majority of workers still have jobs. The British people are now far better off than they were in 1812. So were the Luddites *wrong*? Or just two hundred or so years too early?

We know that technology has advanced tremendously since 1812. What about human beings? Have we advanced as well? In terms of basic biology, we are essentially unchanged. Little if any biological evolution takes place in only two hundred years. Still, doesn't it seem likely that the average British worker today is far more capable than a typical worker nearly two hundred years ago?

Let's imagine what life was like for an average English person in 1812. As it turns out, it's easy to get some insight into this because Charles Dickens was born in that exact year. Dickens drew on his own experiences and observations as a child when he later wrote his famous novels. His descriptions of a harsh, poverty-stricken society and an environment made filthy by the soot from coal-burning industry are well known.

In *Oliver Twist*, Dickens describes the miserable life of an orphan boy during the Industrial Revolution. Here he expresses his feelings as the starving Oliver is given scraps of meat that had first been offered to a dog: "I wish some well-fed philosopher, whose blood is ice, whose heart is iron; could have seen Oliver Twist clutching at the dainty viands the dog had neglected. I wish he could have witnessed the horrible avidity with which Oliver tore the bits asunder with all the ferocity of famine."[15]

Clearly, the average British worker is far better fed today. We know the environment is also much cleaner and more healthy. The literacy rate in Britain today is purported to be as high as 99 percent. It's hard to know what it was in 1812, but around 50 percent might be a decent guess—and of course, the ability to read and write would have been highly concentrated in the upper classes.

In 1812, there was essentially no public education available in England. The government did not begin to invest significantly in education until 1870, and attendance was not compulsory until 1880. Obviously, the average worker today is far better educated than he or she would have been in 1812.

Given all of this, we can say that, due to dramatic improvements in living conditions and education, an average worker today is certainly more capable and able to perform more complex, high-level tasks than a worker in 1812. But the real question is: can we expect that kind of improvement to continue in the future?

The following graph shows what an average worker's ability to perform complex tasks might look like over the past two hundred or so years. The graphic is just an intuitive estimate. It is not based on any real data. However, I suspect that most people would agree with the general shape of the graph, and that is all that really matters.

Average Worker's Ability to Perform Complex Tasks

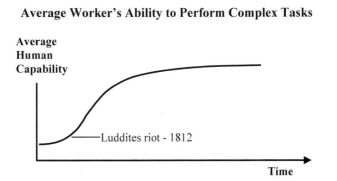

I've chosen an arbitrary point on the graph to indicate the year 1812. After that year, we can reasonably assume that human capability continued to rise quite steeply until we reach modern times. The steep part of the graph reflects dramatic improvements to our overall living conditions in the world's more advanced countries:

- Vastly improved nutrition, public health, and environmental regulations have allowed us to remain relatively free from disease and reach our full biological potential.
- Investment in literacy and in primary and secondary education, as well as access to college and advanced education for some workers, has greatly increased overall capability.
- A generally richer and more varied existence, including easy access to books, media, new technologies and the ability to travel long distances, has probably had a positive impact on our ability to comprehend and deal with complex issues.

The degree of improvement that we have seen, however, is largely related to the low level at which things got started. In education in particular, we seem to have hit a ceiling—and may actually be seeing some evidence of decline. In the United States, the media is replete with a continuing parade of stories about the ongoing crisis in both primary and secondary education.

In the U.S., we are not even sure what the actual high school graduation rate is. A paper published in 2008 by the National Bureau of Economic Research[16] points out that "Depending on the data sources, definitions, and methods used, the U.S. graduation rate has been estimated to be anywhere from 66 to 88 percent in recent years—an astonishingly wide range for such a basic statistic. The range of estimated minority rates is even greater—from 50 to 85 percent." A recently published study by the National Center for Education Statistics[17] showed that over 14 percent of adults in the United States may lack basic reading skills. It seems self evident that if as many as a third of our children are unable to graduate from high school and up to 1/7 of our population fails to achieve basic literacy, then we are *not* succeeding in significantly advancing the capability of the average worker.

Even the earlier trends toward improved nutrition and public health have, in many ways, turned against us. In most Western countries we now have a raging obesity epidemic among the adult population, and—most disturbingly—also among children. While advances in medicine continue, many of these breakthroughs seem to primarily impact the health of retirement-age people. The overall health of our younger population is stagnant or, in some cases, perhaps even declining. In recent years, one of the few positive stories in the public health and nutrition arena has been the decline in the smoking rate.

While the last graph was just an estimate, here is another graph[18] that is based on actual data:

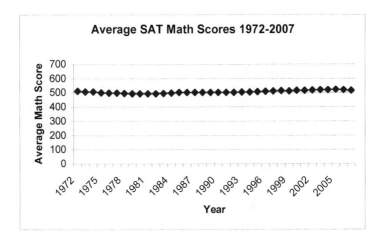

The average math score on SAT tests administered by the College Board has remained essentially flat for the past 35 years. The graph for average verbal scores looks virtually identical. College-bound students that take the SAT are, of course, probably above average in turns of work capability. It seems pretty clear that, in terms of increasing the capability of our average workers, we have already picked the low-hanging fruit, and we are struggling just to maintain things at their current level.

At this point, we should have a pretty good sense that if computer technology continues to progress at the extraordinary rate we have seen in the recent past, then human workers *will not* be able outrun machine capability. You can see this visually with the two graphs below:

Human Capability v. Computer Technology

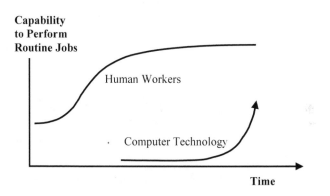

While these two graphs are not based on any specific data, we have shown pretty convincingly that their shape is more or less correct. We know that the lower (computer technology) graph currently lies somewhere below the human average capability graph. And we know that the technology graph is increasing at an exceptionally fast geometric pace. What else do we need to know? Clearly, the lines seem very likely to intersect at some point in the future.[1]

---

[1] If you are familiar with the writings of Thomas Robert Malthus, this graph may look familiar to you. In 1798, Malthus published his *Essays on the Principle of Population* in which he argued that geometrically increasing human population would outstrip society's ability to produce food. In Malthus' version of the graph above, the top (diminishing returns) line represents food production, while the bottom (geometric)

The continuing advance of computer technology along a geometrically increasing path and the diminishing returns from investment in education seem to make a very strong case that the average worker—and perhaps many above-average workers—are in clear danger of having their jobs automated. Next, let's look at some trends and specific technologies that show exactly how this is likely to happen.

Offshoring and Drive-Through Banking

Automation and offshore outsourcing have one important thing in common: they are both driven by technology. Obviously, it is the vast improvement in our communication and information technologies that has enabled many service-oriented jobs to be relocated to low-wage countries.

When I was growing up in the 1970s, I often had the opportunity to see drive-through banking in action. This, of course, was before the introduction of ATM machines. A typical bank drive-through was set up with two or three lanes so that multiple customers could be handled at one time. If you used the lane closest to the building, you

---

line represents population. He believed that the two lines would intersect and result in widespread famine. Malthus, of course, turned out to be wrong largely because he failed to anticipate the technological progress that would occur in food production and processing. So does that mean the graph above is just another "Malthusian" prediction which is also destined to be wrong? One thing to keep in mind is that Malthus in essence placed his bet *against* technology; the graph above assumes exactly the opposite. We should also acknowledge the unhappy possibility that Malthus might still be vindicated in the future, especially if climate change has a highly negative impact on agriculture.

communicated with the teller through a standard cash drawer.

If you were in one of the lanes further out, however, things were far more interesting. You sealed your money, paperwork, checkbook, etc. into a plastic cylinder and then dropped the cylinder into the provided opening. The cylinder then traveled through an underground tube—propelled I think by some sort of vacuum mechanism—until it reached the teller. She then completed the transaction and sent the cylinder back to you the same way. It arrived somewhat like a ball being returned at a bowling alley.

At the time, this seemed very high tech. The system had its flaws, however. I clearly remember waiting in line behind one unlucky bank customer who, failing to insert the cylinder properly, watched it fall to the ground and then roll under his car. He then found that when he attempted to get out and retrieve it, he was unable to open his door. This, of course, was an uproarious sight for an eleven or twelve year old. I would be willing to bet that another potential problem was customers forgetting they still had the cylinder and simply driving away with it.

This type of drive-through bank has now, of course, largely followed in the path of the dinosaurs. Today the technology seems clunky. At the time, however, it represented the leading edge of what was technically possible. Drive- through banks provided a useful convenience to customers and also often offered extended hours of operation.

The point I am making here is that offshoring is really a precursor of automation. Offshoring is what you do when you have *some* technology, but not enough to fully automate a job. Just as clunky drive-through banks were eventually made obsolete by ATMs, so many jobs that are currently being offshored will, in the future, end up being fully automated. This trend was already discernable in 2004, when an article in *InformationWeek* pointed out that "low-wage foreign labor may pose a threat to American call-center workers, but their counterparts in countries such as India and the Philippines themselves face being replaced by increasingly sophisticated voice-automation technology."[19]

This is one of the reasons that I did not include offshoring in our tunnel simulation. We could have simulated an offshored job as an average light flickering out in one part of the tunnel and then another somewhat dimmer light appearing elsewhere. However, our simulation was intended to show what would happen over the long run as automation gradually increased. As technology continues its relentless advance, many of the jobs now being transferred overseas will simply disappear altogether.

Currently, most of the controversy and political debate is focused is on offshoring rather than automation. This may well prove to be a shortsighted view. Information technology (IT) workers in the developed nations have been one of the groups hardest hit by job losses from offshoring. A 2006 study by the Organisation for Economic Co-operation and Development (OECD)[20] concluded that automation has resulted in more IT job losses than offshoring and predicted that this trend will continue. Offshoring is the small wave that distracts you. Automation is the big one further out that you don't see coming.

Short Lived Jobs

The conventional wisdom as generally presented by economists and other analysts is that *technology creates jobs*. While history has shown that this is indeed true, it also shows quite clearly that the new job types created by technology are very often themselves quickly vaporized by the same phenomenon. The IT jobs that are now being offshored and automated are brand new jobs that were largely created in the tech boom of the 1990s. For someone who chose IT as a promising career path little more than ten years ago, this can be a disheartening reality.

Earlier in this chapter, I told of my experience using computer punch cards at the University of Michigan. At the time, these cards were used for nearly everything. The utility bill you received in the mail was often a type of punch card. As a result, there were thousands of "new" jobs for key punch operators. These later became "new" jobs for data entry clerks sitting at computer terminals. Now, of course, technologies such as optical bar codes are greatly reducing the need for this type of data entry.

Similarly, I mentioned that my college field of study, computer engineering, was new at the time. Software engineering is now also a highly offshored field, and much progress has been made toward automating some parts of the software development process. A college student today might well think twice before selecting this relatively new field that was created only about thirty years ago.

Technology has always caused job transitions. Train conductors have been largely replaced by airline flight crews, for example. However, within the high tech and computer fields, the pace of change is unprecedented and continues to drive relentlessly toward the total elimination of jobs. What we are seeing is clear empirical evidence of the geometric increase in the power of computer technology.

Traditional Jobs: The "Average" Lights in the Tunnel

All the attention being focused on new jobs being created by technology tends to distract us from the reality that the bulk of the job types in our economy have remained remarkably stable over time. While technology has certainly impacted the way people in these jobs work, or the types of businesses at which they work, it has not yet altered the basic definitions of these traditional job categories.

The table that follows is constructed from data published by the U.S. Bureau of Labor Statistics in May 2006.[21] It lists all the occupations in the United States with at least one million workers.

U.S. Occupations with at least one million workers (2006)

Occupation	Number of Workers	Percentage of Workers
Retail salespersons	4,374,230	3.3%
Cashiers	3,479,390	2.6%
Office clerks	3,026,710	2.3%
Combined food preparation and serving workers, including fast food	2,461,890	1.9%
Registered nurses	2,417,150	1.8%
Laborers and freight, stock, and material movers, hand	2,372,130	1.8%
Waiters and waitresses	2,312,930	1.7%
Customer service representatives	2,147,770	1.6%
Janitors and cleaners, except maids and housekeeping cleaners	2,124,860	1.6%
Bookkeeping, accounting, and auditing clerks	1,856,890	1.4%
Secretaries, except legal, medical, and executive	1,750,600	1.3%
Stock clerks and order fillers	1,705,450	1.3%
Truck drivers, heavy and tractor-trailer	1,673,950	1.3%
General and operations managers	1,663,280	1.3%
Elementary school teachers	1,509,180	1.1%
Sales representatives, wholesale and manufacturing, except technical and scientific products	1,488,990	1.1%

Executive secretaries and administrative assistants	1,487,310	1.1%
Nursing aides, orderlies, and attendants	1,376,660	1.0%
First-line supervisors/managers of office and administrative support workers	1,351,180	1.0%
Maintenance and repair workers, general	1,310,580	1.0%
Team assemblers	1,250,120	0.9%
Teacher assistants	1,246,030	0.9%
Receptionists and information clerks	1,112,350	0.8%
First-line supervisors/managers of retail sales workers	1,111,740	0.8%
Accountants and auditors	1,092,960	0.8%
Secondary school teachers, except special and vocational education	1,030,780	0.8%
Construction laborers	1,016,530	0.8%
Security guards	1,004,130	0.8%
Total of Occupations Listed Above	*50,755,770*	*38.3%*
All Other Occupations	*81,849,210*	*61.7%*
Total Employment	**132,604,980**	**100.0%**

These workers make up a significant number of the average lights that we automated away in our simulation. Where are the "new" jobs created by technology? I can find exactly one job mentioned in this list which could not have existed in 1930. Can you find it? Give up? Four lines from the top it says "including fast food." McDonalds didn't introduce the fast food concept until 1948.

The job types listed in the table make up nearly 40 percent of all the workers in the United States. Each of us could probably also come up with dozens of other job titles that have similarly remained unchanged for half a century or more. Many of these are much higher paying professional jobs: doctors, dentists, CPAs, lawyers, architects, pilots, engineers, etc. The fact is that the vast majority of our workers continue to be employed in traditional jobs. The new job types created by technology represent a relatively small fraction of employment and, as noted above, often tend not to last very long.

Even within high technology industries, the bulk of jobs are traditional jobs. Suppose you found a new technology start-up company in Silicon Valley. You obtain funding, and your company starts to grow. Who do you hire? Engineers, people to work in accounting, human resources, marketing and finance; administrative assistants and people to work in shipping and receiving: these are all traditional jobs. The people working at Google do not all have weird new-age jobs; by and large, they have the same types of jobs as people working at General Motors. What needs to concern us is not just the *number* of new jobs created by technology, but the *types* of jobs. Later in this chapter, we will see that entire traditional job categories are at risk of being heavily automated in the not too distant future. To suggest that technology is going to somehow create completely new job categories capable of absorbing millions of workers displaced from traditional jobs is pure fantasy.

What are the implications for our economy if a large fraction of these traditional jobs are ultimately automated away? Automated checkout lanes are currently in use at a number of retail stores. We can be sure that in the future, these will become more reliable, easier to use, and more popular. What will we do if someday a substantial percentage of the three and a half million cashiers in the U.S. no longer have jobs? What additional education and training can we offer these workers? And what jobs would it prepare them for?

And what is the impact of that potential unemployment on market demand for goods and services? Cashiers are generally not highly paid, but they nonetheless exist as lights in our mass market tunnel. Cashiers, just like other workers, drive cars, buy clothes and consumer electronics, rent DVDs, shop for Christmas gifts and perhaps drink coffee at Starbucks. In terms of *unit* demand for moderately priced personal products like cell phones or mp3 players, a cashier may count as much as a corporate CEO.

Many of the jobs listed in the table are already in the process of being automated or offshored. Others will be targeted in the very near future. Millions of other workers in occupations that do not appear in the list are also at high risk. As we will see, this includes many occupations that are not, by any means, either low-skill or low paid. Allowing these jobs to be relentlessly eliminated by the millions, without any concrete plan to handle the issues that will result, is a clear recipe for disaster.

A Tale of Two Jobs

A common misconception about automation is the idea that it will primarily impact low paying jobs that require few skills or training. To illustrate that this is not necessarily the case, consider two very different occupations: a radiologist and a housekeeper.

A radiologist is a medical doctor who specializes in interpreting images generated by various medical scanning technologies. Before the advent of modern computer technology, radiologists focused exclusively on X-rays. This has now been expanded to include all types of medical imaging, including CT scans, PET scans, mammograms, etc. To become a radiologist you need to attend college for four years, and then medical school for another four. That is followed by another five years of internship and residency, and often even more specialized training after that. Radiology is one the most popular specialties for newly minted doctors because it offers relatively high pay and regular work hours; radiologists generally don't need to work weekends or handle emergencies.

In spite of the radiologist's training requirement of at least thirteen additional years beyond high school, it is conceptually quite easy to envision this job being automated. The primary focus of the job is to analyze and evaluate visual images. Furthermore, the parameters of each image are highly defined since they are often coming directly from a computerized scanning device.

Visual pattern recognition software is a rapidly developing field that has already produced significant results. The government currently has access to software that can help identify terrorists in airports based on visual analysis of security photographs.[22] Real world tasks such as this are probably technically more difficult than analyzing a medical scan because the environment and objects in the image are far more varied.

Radiology is already subject to significant offshoring to India and other places. It is a simple matter to transmit digital scans to an overseas location for analysis. Indian doctors earn as little as 10 percent of what American radiologists are paid.[23] As we saw earlier, automation will often come rapidly on the heels of offshoring, especially if the job focuses purely on technical analysis with little need for human interaction. Currently, U.S. demand for radiologists continues to expand because of the increase in use of diagnostic scans such as mammograms. However, this seems likely to slow as automation and offshoring advance and become bigger players in the future. The graduating medical students who are now rushing into radiology for its high pay and relative freedom from the annoyances of dealing with actual patients may eventually come to question the wisdom of their decision.

Now let's turn to a very different job: that of a housekeeper. A housekeeper, of course, doesn't require any formal education at all, but as you might have guessed, this job is actually much harder to fully automate than the radiologist's. To take over the housekeeping job, we would need to build a very advanced robot—or perhaps several robots to perform various tasks.

If you asked the housekeeper to name the most difficult part of his or her job, you might expect the answer to be cleaning the bathrooms or the windows. For our robot, however, the truly difficult task is probably something that is relatively light work for the human housekeeper. Consider what is involved in tidying up clutter in a typical home. For the housekeeper, this is easy. A human being can instantly recognize objects that are out of place and can quickly put them back where they belong. Building a machine to reliably do the same thing is probably one of the most difficult challenges in robotics.

A housekeeping robot would need to be able to recognize hundreds or even thousands of objects that belong in the average home and know where they belong. In addition, it would need to figure out what to do with an almost infinite variety of new objects that might be brought in from outside.

Designing computer software capable of recognizing objects in a very complex and variable field of view and then controlling a robot arm to correctly manipulate those objects is extraordinarily difficult. The task is made even more challenging by the fact that the objects could be in many possible orientations or configurations. Consider the simple case of a pair of sunglasses sitting on a table. The sunglasses might be closed with the lenses facing down, or with the lenses up. Or perhaps the glasses are open with the lenses oriented vertically. Or maybe one side of the glasses is open and the other closed. And, of course, the glasses could be rotated in any direction. And perhaps they are touching or somehow entangled with other objects. Building and programming a robot that is able to recognize the sunglasses in any possible configuration and then pick them up, fold them and put them back in their case is so difficult that we can probably conclude that the house-keeper's job is relatively safe for the time being.

Contrast the housekeeping robot's complex visual recognition challenge with the task of automating the radiologist's job. A medical scan is, by definition, precise in terms of its scale and orientation: you know exactly what you are looking at. You don't need to worry about dealing with unknown objects oriented in different ways. In fact, the entire point may be simply to locate something out of the ordinary, such as a tumor. It is also much easier and more profitable to partially automate the radiologist's job. There would be little point to building a housekeeping robot that could only clear up some of the clutter in a home. On the other hand, if you can automate 20 percent of the radiologist's more routine work, then you can immediately eliminate one out of five radiology jobs.

None of this is to say that the housekeeper's job will never be automated. It is very likely that intense research and development in robotics will eventually produce a solution to even the most difficult problems. In addition, robots already exist to automate a few of the housekeeper's more routine tasks. You can already purchase inexpensive robot vacuum cleaners, and larger industrial floor cleaning robots are also available. As *The Economist* pointed out in June 2008, "Robots are getting cleverer and more dexterous. Their time has almost come." [24]

Still, it seems likely that the radiologist's job is at higher risk of being automated in the near future.[*] A big part of the reason for this is that the radiologist has what I call a *software job*.

"Software" Jobs and Artificial Intelligence

When I speak of a "software" job, I don't mean that a person who has the job necessarily works with or programs software. I simply mean that automation of the job potentially requires only sufficiently advanced software. In other words, someone with a software job could eventually be replaced by a computer similar to the one that currently sits on his or her desk. There is no need for robotic arms or, in fact, any moving parts at all. Another, more common, term for people with software jobs is, of course, *knowledge worker*.

Software jobs are also highly subject to offshoring. The conventional wisdom used to be that becoming a

---

[*] In reality, there is another factor that might slow the adoption of full automation in Radiology: that is malpractice liability. Because the result of a mistake or oversight in reading a medical scan would likely be dire for the patient, the maker of a completely automated system would assume huge potential liability in the event of errors. This liability, of course, also exists for radiologists, but it is distributed across thousands of doctors. However, it is certainly possible that legislation and/or court decisions will largely remove this barrier in the future. For example, in February 2008, the U.S. Supreme Court ruled in an 8-1 decision that, in certain cases, medical device manufacturers are protected from product liability cases as long as the FDA has approved the device. In general, we can expect that non-technological factors such as product liability or the power of organized labor will slow automation in certain fields, but the overall trend will remain relentless.

knowledge worker represented the best path to a prosperous future. The advent of offshoring has increasingly called this proposition into question. Today, offshoring is impacting knowledge workers across the board. Jobs in fields such as radiology, accounting, tax preparation, graphic design, and especially all types of information technology are already being shipped to India and to other countries. This trend will only grow, and as I have pointed out previously, where offshoring appears, automation is often likely to eventually follow.

The automation of software jobs is tied closely to the field of artificial intelligence. When most of us think about artificial intelligence, we are quickly sidetracked into the world of science fiction. We think of the robots C3PO and R2D2 from the *Star Wars* movies, or perhaps the HAL 2000 computer from *2001: A Space Odyssey*. As a result of this, we have been lured into the false belief that in order to replace us, machines have to become like us— that, in fact, they have to somehow replicate our humanity.

This is simply not true. How often has each of us said "I am not my job." Or "I work to live; not the other way around." How much of your complete identity as a human being really goes into your job? Outside of work, you may read books; listen to a certain type of music. Maybe you have a hobby or passion. Perhaps you feel strongly about politics or the environment. Certainly you care deeply for your children, your family and others close to you. Collectively, all this makes up who you are. Duplicating all of that in a machine certainly remains in the realm of science fiction. *But how much of all that is really required to do your job?*

The fact is that the bar which technology needs to hurdle in order to displace many of us in the workplace is much lower than we really imagine.

To gain some insight into how artificial intelligence works in the real world, let's consider computer chess. In 1989, Garry Kasparov, the world chess champion faced off against a special computer called Deep Thought. Deep Thought was designed at Carnegie Mellon University and IBM. Kasparov easily defeated the machine in a two game match.

In 1996, Kasparov faced a new computer developed by IBM called Deep Blue. Again Kasparov defeated the computer. In 1997, IBM came back with an improved version of Deep Blue that finally defeated Kasparov in a six game match. This represented the first time that a machine had defeated the top human chess player.

Since then, computer chess has continued to progress. In 2006, the new world chess champion, Vladimir Kramnik, lost a match against a German software program called Deep Fritz. While IBM's Deep Blue was a completely custom computer about the size of a refrigerator, Deep Fritz is a program that runs on a computer using two standard Intel processors. It seems highly likely that, in the near future, a program like Deep Fritz, running on virtually any cheap laptop computer, will be able to defeat the best chess players in the world.

When we think of what it takes for a human being to be a world chess champion, most of us would probably agree that it takes a certain degree of creativity—at least within the confines of a highly defined set of rules. Yet, creativity is a trait that we are very reluctant to ascribe to a machine—even if that machine can beat a human at chess. This tendency to be somewhat underwhelmed by the accomplishments of machines, may have something to do with the fact that the working of the human brain remains a mystery.

Who can say what is going on in a human chess master's head when he or she plays a match? We simply don't know. And therefore it becomes to us something mysterious and especially creative. In the case of the computer, however, we know exactly what is happening. The computer is simply calculating through millions of different possible moves and then picking the best one. It is using a *brute force* algorithm. The computer's advantage arises not from the fact that it is genuinely smart, but because it is almost unimaginably fast. It's natural for us to give this brute force accomplishment a lower status than the creativity and precise thinking exhibited by an exceptional human being. But the question for us here is: will that protect us from brute force algorithms that can do our jobs?

If you agree that the game of chess requires creativity within a set of defined rules, then could not something similar be said about the field of law? Currently there are jobs in the United States for many thousands of lawyers who rarely, if ever, go into a courtroom. These attorneys are employed in the areas of legal research and contracts. They work at law firms and spend much of their time in the library or accessing legal databases through their computers. They research case law, and write briefs which summarize relevant court cases and legal strategies from the past. They review contracts and look for loopholes. They suggest possible strategies and legal arguments for new cases that come to their firms.

Based on our previous discussion, the first thing you might guess about these attorneys is that they are already subject to offshoring. And you would be correct: in India there are already teams of lawyers who specialize in researching case law not in India—but in the United States.

What about automation? Can a computer do the lawyer's job? One of the primary research areas in artificial intelligence has focused on creating "smart" algorithms that can quickly search, evaluate and summarize information. We see the fruition of this body of research every time we use Google or any other advanced Internet search engine. We can expect that such smart algorithms will increasingly be used in the field of legal research. The software may start out as a productivity tool to make the lawyer's job easier, and then eventually evolve into a full automation solution.

Obviously, it is easier to automate some parts of the lawyer's job than others. For example, finding and summarizing relevant case law would be a likely target for an initial effort. As I pointed out with the radiologist, automating even a portion of the lawyer's job will quickly result in fewer attorneys on the payroll. What about the more advanced or creative aspects of the lawyer's job? Could a computer formulate a strategy for an important legal case? For the time being, this may be a challenge, but as we saw in the case of chess, a brute force algorithm may ultimately prevail. If a computer can evaluate millions of possible chess moves, then why can it not also iterate through every known legal argument since the days when Cicero held forth in the Roman Forum? Would this be a "lesser" form of legal creativity? Perhaps it would. But would that matter to our lawyer's employer?

Although the practical applications of artificial intelligence have so far emphasized brute force solutions, it is by no means true that this is the only approach being taken in the field. A very important area of study revolves around the idea of *neural nets*, which are a special type of computer that is built upon a model of the human brain. Neural nets are currently being used in areas such as visual pattern recognition. In the future, we can probably expect some important advances in this area, especially as the engineers who design neural nets work more closely with scientists who are uncovering the secrets of how our brains work.

One thing that probably jumps out at you as we speak of lawyers and radiologists is that these people make a lot of money. The average radiologist in the United States makes over $300,000. In fact, we can reasonably say that software jobs (or knowledge worker jobs) are typically high paying jobs. This creates a very strong incentive for businesses to offshore and, when possible, automate these jobs. Another point we can make is that there is really no relationship between how much training is required for a human being, and how difficult it is to automate the job. To become a lawyer or a radiologist requires both college and graduate degrees, but this will not hold off automation. It is a relatively simple matter to program accumulated knowledge into an algorithm or enter it into a database.

For knowledge workers, there is really a double dose of bad news. Not only are their jobs potentially easier to automate than other job types because no investment in mechanical equipment is required; but also, the financial incentive for getting rid of the job is significantly higher. As a result, we can expect that, in the future, automation will fall heavily on knowledge workers and in particular on highly paid workers. In cases where technology is not yet sufficient to automate the job, offshoring is likely to be pursued as an interim solution.

Given this reality, it may be that the simulation we performed in Chapter 1 was actually somewhat conservative. Look back at the table listing traditional jobs on page 59. Very few of these people are knowledge workers. In our simulation, we assumed that automation would fall evenly on some significant percentage of the average lights in the tunnel. We now see, however, that automation may, in fact, arrive in a relatively "top heavy" pattern. It may well be that a great many of the brighter lights in our tunnel will be among the first impacted.

What does this mean for a business that offers products and services in the mass market? Clearly, it implies that automation may be poised to someday eliminate not just untold millions of your potential customers—it is likely to hit hard at your *best* customers.

Automation, Offshoring and Small Business

We tend to think of automation and offshoring as primarily impacting jobs in large corporations. After all, it takes a substantial investment to set up a relationship with an overseas outsourcing firm or bring in specialized automation equipment or software. In the near future, however, both of these practices are likely to become increasing accessible and inexpensive for even the smallest businesses.

There is a significant trend toward breaking jobs into smaller pieces or specific tasks—which can then be either automated or offshored. This capability is increasingly being offered to small businesses either as pre-packaged software or through easy to use online interfaces over the Internet. Tax preparation is one area where this approach is already widespread. Instead of making a large investment in sophisticated automation software, a small business owner or manager will be able to visit a website and then rent access to the software on either a per-hour or per-task basis. I think it is very possible that the same will happen with task-specific offshoring. Competition between service providers will quickly produce lower prices, easier to use online interfaces, and a wider variety of services.

The result will be rapid penetration of these practices into businesses of all sizes. As we saw with the radiologist and the lawyer, once significant portions of jobs can be automated, the number of workers employed will immediately begin to fall. The U.S. Small Business Administration estimates that businesses with fewer than 500 employees have generated from 60-80 percent of all job growth over the past decade.[25] As it becomes easier and cheaper for business owners to employ automation and offshoring, we may well find that these practices will become a significant drag on America's primary job creation engine.

"Hardware" Jobs and Robotics

A "hardware" job is a job that requires some investment in mechanical or robotic technologies in order for the job to be automated. The automation of hardware jobs started long before the computer revolution. Machines used on assembly lines, farm equipment, and heavy earth moving equipment are all technologies that have displaced millions of workers in the past. As history has shown, repetitive motion manufacturing jobs are among the easiest to automate. In fact, as I mentioned, this is how the Luddite movement got started back in 1811. However, the merger of mechanics and computer technology into the field of robotics will almost certainly impact an unprecedented number and types of jobs. Whether a specific hardware job is difficult or easy to automate really depends on the combination of skills and manual dexterity required.

For an example of a job that is very difficult to automate, let's consider an auto mechanic. A mechanic obviously requires a great deal of hand-eye coordination. He or she has to work on thousands of different parts in a variety of different engines, often in highly varied states of repair. In other words, a robot mechanic would face many visual recognition and manipulation problems similar to the ones we discussed earlier with the robot housekeeper. In addition, the robot mechanic would require a much higher degree of problem solving skill than the housekeeper. In fact, this diagnostic skill is not something that could be solved with software alone because it extends to nearly all the human senses. A mechanic may listen to the sound an engine makes or even diagnose a problem based on a specific smell.

As things stand, we can say that becoming an auto mechanic is probably a pretty safe choice for the time being. But, as we said with the housekeeper, that does not imply the job will be safe forever. Advances in robotic technology will continue relentlessly until many of these problems are solved. However, an even more important factor is likely to be changes made to the cars the mechanic is working on. Advancing technology has already impacted the way mechanics work; computerized diagnostic tools are now used to read fault codes provided by microprocessors embedded in the engine. We can expect that this trend will continue, and that, at some point in the future, cars may well be designed specifically to be worked on by robotic mechanics.

A truck driver is another example of a job that is likely to be protected for the time being, but, in the long run, the reason will probably not be so much technology as social acceptance. The military is already making substantial investments in automated trucks that could be used on the battlefield. These could be completely autonomous, or they might be programmed to simply follow a lead truck. Similarly, many car manufacturers will soon be deploying collision avoidance technology in cars. These systems will help drivers avoid mistakes that might lead to accidents; however over time they could evolve into technology capable of driving the car autonomously—just as jet airliners now routinely fly and land without assistance.

While the technology for automated cars and trucks may arrive, it is somewhat difficult to imagine that most people would be eager to share the road with 50-ton driverless trucks. A second important issue would likely be the power of the Teamsters union. Once again, however, I have to give my standard disclaimer: this does not mean truck driving jobs will always be protected.

The job types that are likely to be threatened fairly soon by advances in robotics are the jobs that fit somewhere between the auto mechanic and the repetitive motion assembly line worker. As an example, consider the shelf stocker in a supermarket or chain retail store. This job requires more flexibility than working on an assembly line, but still falls far short of what the auto mechanic faces.

The layout of a supermarket is standardized and could easily be programmed into a computer. The aisles are wide and the floors are smooth; ideal territory for an industrial robot. Every item has a specific place on the shelves. Bar codes make it a simple matter to identify items, and special location markers could be placed on the shelves: a shelf stocking robot faces few of the visual recognition issues that challenged our housekeeping or auto mechanic robots. Designing a robot that could move inventory from the stock room and place it on shelves is certainly well within the realm of possibility in the not too distant future. Needless to say, if a robot can be designed to stock shelves, then it can also be made to unload trucks and move material of all types.

Skeptical that robots might someday be stepping into these jobs? Consider that as far back as 2005, *CNET News Blog* published an article entitled "Why so Nervous about robots, Wal-Mart?"[26] The article pointed out that reports had surfaced about Wal-Mart testing inventory-taking robots. These would be robots programmed to navigate the aisles at night and automatically take a complete store inventory. When the CNET reporter contacted Wal-Mart management, he received an unusually abrupt denial that Wal-Mart was considering using robots in any way.

We can take Wal-Mart's management at its word and assume that it, in fact, has no plans to use robots. In the long run, however, that won't matter. At some point, if one of Wal-Mart's competitors tries to gain an advantage by employing robots, then Wal-Mart and every other competing business will really have no choice but to follow suit. The point of this is not to vilify Wal-Mart or any other business that might someday choose to employ automation. We have to acknowledge that, in a free market economy, every business has to respond to its competitive environment and employ the best available technologies and processes. If it does not do so, it will not survive.

History has shown that job automation very often involves pushing a significant portion of the job onto the customer. Automation in the customer service area is really *self-service*. This has been the case with ATMs, automated checkout aisles and even self-serve gas pumps. In the recently opened Future Store[27] near Düsseldorf, Germany, in-store retail sales and customer assistance is being automated via a cell-phone interface. Shoppers are able to get real time assistance, while shopping, through their mobile phones. They can also scan bar codes as they shop and, in the near future, will be able to pay for their purchases directly through their phones—presumably avoiding the checkout aisle altogether.

The specter of near fully automated supermarkets and chain retail stores is cause for genuine concern. These are now the jobs of last resort. These are the jobs that workers displaced from other industries take because there is nothing better available. Look back at the table on page 59. We have already mentioned that 3.5 million cashiers are potentially at risk. The table shows another 4 million retail salespersons and 2.3 million laborers and freight, stock and material movers, as well as 1.7 million stock clerks and order fillers. What new jobs could we possibly find for all these people?

Read any article in the popular press about the field of robotics and its potential future implications, and you will almost invariably find a sentence pointing out that "in the future, robots will be used to perform tasks which are dangerous for people, or jobs which people don't really want." That is surely true, but it implies the somewhat wistful assumption that robots *won't* be used in jobs that people *do* want. That is obviously a silly assumption. Robots, and other forms of automation, will be used instead of people as soon it becomes cost effective and profitable for businesses to do so.[1]

---

[1] For more on robotics and its potential impact on employment and on society, see Marshall Brain's "Robotic Nation" blog at http://roboticnation.blogspot.com.

"Interface" Jobs

A third type of job is what I call an "interface" job. The people who hold these jobs, to a large extent, fill in the cracks which currently exist between various information formats and technologies. As an example, consider what happens when you apply for a home mortgage loan. If you work with an independent mortgage agent, he or she will probably give you a paper application to fill out. Next, you will need to retrieve and make copies of your supporting documentation: pay stubs, tax returns, bank statements, insurance documents, etc.

All of this documentation will be on paper or it will be faxed to you. A property appraisal will be done, and the report will be forwarded to the loan agent. Once the loan agent collects everything together, he or she will probably fax it all to the bank, where a loan officer will review it. Ultimately, numbers such as your salary, credit rating, and the equity to loan ratio will be plugged into a computer program and the loan will either be approved or denied.

Clearly, the bulk of the labor associated with this process is in collecting, copying, collating and faxing information. The intellectual portion of the job—either approving or denying the loan—is probably already essentially handled by a computer. Throughout the economy, there are probably thousands of jobs for clerks and office workers that continue to exist because of this clunky interface between what exists on paper and what needs to be in a computer.

Clearly, we cannot expect that this state of affairs will continue forever. Financial statements are already available online. Standard data formats are making it increasingly easy for computers to talk directly to one another. The "XML" standard is a very popular format that is already widely used to move data between different businesses over the Internet. Using XML, the computers at a manufacturing company can talk directly to the computers belonging to the company's suppliers. The continuing drive toward paperless documents and seamless communication is likely to eliminate many of these human interface jobs in the coming years.

The Next "Killer App"

Since the beginnings of the personal computer industry, computer hardware sales have often been driven by a particular software application so compelling that it has motivated customers to purchase the machine required to run it. When the Apple II was introduced in 1977, it was initially a success within a relatively small group of computer hobbyists. It wasn't until the first electronic spreadsheet, VisiCalc, was developed that the Apple II began to generate wider interest. VisiCalc was the catalyst that helped transform the Apple II from an interesting toy into a true business machine. Likewise, when the IBM PC was introduced, Lotus 1-2-3 fulfilled the "killer app" role. Later, it was graphic design and desktop publishing software that drove the Apple MacIntosh to success.

In recent years, the highest sales growth for the computer industry has not been in high-end desktop computers but instead in laptops and, lately, the newer netbook machines that provide a simple and inexpensive way to browse the web. At least in part, this probably results from the fact that the acceleration of computer hardware capability has largely outpaced what is required to run most of the software applications of interest to the average user. If you are primarily interested in word processing, spreadsheets and web browsing, it may be difficult to justify the cost of a high-end computer when a lower cost or more portable machine offers more than enough power to run the software. Likewise, it seems to be increasingly difficult for Microsoft and other software vendors to continually add new features to desktop productivity applications and operating systems that are compelling enough to justify expensive upgrades.

Yet the business models of both Intel and Microsoft depend on continuing to sell ever more powerful processors and new or updated software applications to take advantage of that power. If customers were to permanently turn away from the idea of faster processors, the business would quickly become commoditized, and Intel would lose its competitive advantage. For that reason, we can be sure that Intel, Microsoft and hundreds of other software companies are actively seeking the next killer app—something that will fully leverage the vastly increased computer power that will be available in the coming years and decades.

I think that there are good reasons to believe that this next killer app is going to turn out to be artificial intelligence (AI). AI applications are highly compute intensive and will take full advantage of all the computational power that new processors can offer. New standalone AI applications will appear, but more importantly, artificial intelligence is likely to be built directly into existing productivity applications and operating systems, as well as the enterprise software and database systems used by large businesses.

The market for AI software is likely to extend far beyond the computer industry. Increasingly sophisticated robots will demand the most advanced hardware and software available. High-end microprocessors and AI software will also surely be used to build intelligence into appliances, consumer devices and industrial equipment of all kinds. Ultimately, robots and other non-computer applications may well eclipse the personal computer market as the primary growth engine for leading-edge hardware and software.

Products that give some insight into what the future may hold are already on display. Microsoft recently demonstrated a "virtual personal assistant" which appears as a computer generated person on the screen. The assistant is capable of tasks such as making airline reservations or scheduling meetings and requires the most advanced hardware available. According to the *New York Times*, Microsoft's virtual assistant can "make sophisticated decisions about the people in front of her, judging things like their attire, whether they seem impatient, their importance and their preferred times for appointments."[28] The *Times* article also quotes a Microsoft executive who speculates that future applications might include a "medical doctor in a box" that could help with basic medical issues.

An artificial intelligence application that could dispense basic medical advice is certainly a compelling idea, especially in light of the continuing problem with accelerating health care costs. However, it raises an important point. What education and training would we require of a *person* who dispensed such information? Would this person need to be a doctor? Perhaps not, but clearly this would not be one of the low skill, low wage jobs that we often associate with vulnerability to automation. The reality is that there is simply little or no relationship between the level of education and training required for a person to do a job and whether or not that job can be automated. While doctors are probably not in danger of losing their jobs in the foreseeable future, the same cannot be said for many thousands of knowledge workers and middle managers in the private sector.

It's important to note that, while humanoid interfaces like Microsoft's virtual assistant make for great demonstrations, the AI applications that will likely displace knowledge workers will not need such elaborate interfaces. They will simply be workhorse programs that make the routine decisions and perform the tasks and analysis that are currently the responsibility of highly paid workers sitting in cubicles all over the world. AI capability may start out by being built into the productivity applications used by workers, but over time, it will evolve to the point that these applications can perform much of the work autonomously: AI will become a tool for managers rather than workers. The result is likely to be substantial job losses for knowledge workers and a flattening of organizational charts that will eliminate large numbers of middle managers. (The impact of automation will, of course, be in addition to that of offshoring.) Many of these people will be highly educated professionals who had previously assumed that they were, because of their skills and advanced educations, beneficiaries of the trend toward an increasingly technological and globalized world.'

Military Robotics

One of the biggest investors in robotics technology is the Pentagon. In his recent book *Wired for War: The Robotics Revolution and Conflict in the 21st Century*, P.W. Singer points out that the U.S. military expects robotic technologies to play an increasingly important role in conflicts of the future. Remote-controlled drone aircraft and bomb-defusing ground robots are already making crucial contributions to the war effort in Iraq and Afghanistan. The Defense Advanced Research Projects Agency (DARPA)—the birthplace of the original computer network that led to the Internet—now considers military robotics to be one of its top research priorities.[29] In the coming decades, we can anticipate far more advanced robots playing an increasingly autonomous role in warfare in the air, on the ground and at sea.

All of this makes for a rather harsh contrast between the foresight shown by the military as compared with civilian economists and analysts. Consider the uneven terrain and the highly unpredictable and dynamic situations that

---

' Please see "Machine Intelligence and the Turing Test" in the Appendix for more on artificial intelligence.

would be faced by battlefield robots. Now compare that with the environment inside a supermarket or warehouse. It seems obvious that designing robots to perform much of the routine work required within commercial and industrial job settings is far less challenging than producing autonomous military robots. The U.S. military is rightly investing substantial resources in studying the future impact of robotics and artificial intelligence on the way in which future wars will be fought. And yet, little or no cohesive thought or planning is being given to the disruptive impact that these technologies will certainly have in the commercial sector and on the overall economy.

Robotics and Offshoring

As we've shown, "software" jobs are highly subject to offshoring and potentially also to automation. Those "Hardware" jobs that require significant hand-eye coordination in a varied environment are currently very difficult to fully automate. But what about offshoring? Can a hardware job be offshored?

In fact it can, and we are likely to see this increasingly in the near future. As an example, consider a manufacturing assembly line. Suppose that the highly repetitive jobs have already been automated, but there remain jobs for skilled operators at certain key points in the production process. How could management get rid of these skilled workers?

They could simply build a remote controlled robot to perform the task, and then offshore the control function. As we have pointed out, it is the ability to recognize a complex visual image and then manipulate a robot arm based on that image that is a primary challenge preventing full robotic automation. Transmitting a real-time visual image overseas, where a low paid worker can then manipulate the machinery, is certainly already feasible. Remote controlled robots are currently used in military and police applications that would be dangerous for humans. We very likely will see such robots in factories and workplaces in the near future.

Nanotechnology and its Impact on Employment

One of the most exciting and high impact technological advances that we can look forward to in the coming decades is in the emerging field of *nanotechnology*. Nanotechnology is concerned with the manipulation of matter at the molecular or even the atomic level. In the future, we may be able to build molecular machines: tiny inventions, far smaller than the head of a pin, that can essentially transform matter and create nearly anything we want out of the most basic ingredients.

This may seem like pure fantasy until we learn that nanotechnology is already here and has been operating since long before human beings walked the earth.[1] It is all around us and even inside us. All living things, at the most basic level, operate under the direction of molecular ma-

---

[1] I am referring here to truly advanced nanotechnology or "molecular machines." A number of techniques and processes which are currently in use are referred to as "nanotechnology," but these really represent the leading edge of traditional materials science. It is likely to be decades before advanced nanotechnology is put to widespread, practical use.

chines. We know that our genetic recipe is encoded in the double helix-shaped DNA molecules in the nucleus of our cells. But how does that recipe get translated into an incomprehensibly complex organism like a human being?

If we could zoom in and watch the action inside our cells, we would see tiny molecular machines "unzip" our DNA molecules and read portions of our genetic code in a way that is not unlike a computer scanning in a bar code. That genetic "bar code" is then transmitted to another area in our cells. In a tiny biological factory called the ribosome, the recipe captured in the bar code is again read by other nano-machines that build protein molecules. It is these protein molecules that are the true building blocks of life. Our muscle tissue, the hemoglobin in our red blood cells, the insulin that we need to process sugar, the enzymes that digest our food—all of these and countless thousands of other structures and chemicals that comprise our bodies and make us function are proteins. And they are all constructed through nanotechnology.

It is likely that the coming "nanotech" revolution will begin with the study of these existing, living machines. Imagine a team of scientists descending on an alien spacecraft found buried in the New Mexico desert. They would begin by studying this alien technology and attempting to reverse-engineer it. In time, they might begin to tinker with the spacecraft and make it operate in new and different ways. Eventually, they would understand the technology at a fundamental level, and they would begin using it to build new machines of their own. This will quite probably be the path along which nanotechnology will evolve.[30]

Nanotechnology is currently in its infancy, and it is likely that it will take decades before truly advanced applications become available. Nonetheless, the field offers enormous promise and may someday touch nearly every aspect of our lives. Amazing new treatments and cures in the field of medicine, the possibility of generating virtually limitless energy from the sun, even faster and more powerful computers, unimaginable new possibilities in manufacturing—all these things and more may come from nanotechnology.

But as we contemplate these exciting possibilities, there is another question we need to ask: will nanotechnology create jobs? Will our displaced cashiers and shelf-stockers and office clerks find employment in the nanotechnology industry? A simple application of common sense should give us the answer. We speak here of manipulating matter at the molecular level. The level of precision required is obviously beyond any human being, and nanotechnology will have to be fully automated. Certainly there may be jobs for a few very highly trained technicians, but the idea that jobs will be created for blue collar workers is fantasy. If in fact, at some point in the future, the bulk of our traditional manufacturing evolves into nano-manufacturing, the global impact on employment would be nearly beyond measure.

The Future of College Education

Nearly everyone agrees that a college degree is generally a ticket to a brighter future. In the United States in 2006, the average worker with a bachelor's degree earned $56,788,[31] while the average high school graduate earned a little more than half this amount, or \$31,071. Workers with graduate or professional degrees earned a still higher average salary of \$82,320. While the primary motive for the majority of individuals to pursue advanced education is almost certainly economic, we would all agree that education also conveys many other benefits both to the individual and to society as a whole. A person with more education seems likely to enjoy a generally richer existence, to have an interest in a greater variety of issues and is perhaps also more likely to be focused on continuing personal and professional growth. A more educated society is generally a more civil society with a lower crime rate. An educated person is likely to hang out in the library—rather than on street corners.

The unfortunate reality, however, is that the college dream is likely at some point to collide with the trends in offshoring and automation that we have been discussing in this chapter. The fact is that college graduates very often end up taking "software" jobs; they become knowledge workers. As we have seen, these jobs—and in particular more routine or entry level jobs—are at very high risk. The danger is that as these trends accelerate, a college degree will be seen increasingly not as a ticket to a prosperous future, but as a ticket to a job that will very likely vaporize. At some point in the future, the high cost of a college education, together with diminishing prospects for college graduates, is likely to begin having a negative impact on college enrollment. This will be especially true of students coming from more modest backgrounds, but it will have impact at all levels of society.

This is, obviously, a very unconventional view. Most economists and others who study such trends would probably strongly argue exactly the opposite case: that in the future, a college degree will be increasingly valuable and there will be strong demand for well-educated workers.

This is essentially the "skill premium" argument—the idea that technology is creating jobs for highly skilled workers even as it destroys opportunities for the unskilled. I think the evidence clearly shows that this has indeed been the case over the past couple of decades, but I do not think it can continue indefinitely. The reason is simple: machines and computers are advancing in capability and will increasingly invade the realm of the highly educated. We'll likely see evidence of this at some point in the form of diminished opportunity and unemployment among recent graduates and also among older college-educated workers who lose jobs and are unable to find comparable positions.

We may not see an actual closing of the gap in average pay for college v. non-college graduates because opportunities for workers of all skill levels are likely to be in decline. I am not suggesting that high school graduates who would have otherwise gone to college will choose to remain completely unskilled, but I do think there is likely to be a migration toward relatively skilled blue collar jobs if there is a perception that these occupations offer more security.

As new high school graduates begin to shy away from a course leading to knowledge worker jobs, they will increasingly turn to the trades. As we have seen, jobs for people like auto mechanics, truck drivers, plumbers and so forth are among the most difficult to automate. The result may well be intense competition for these relatively "safe" jobs. As high school graduates who might previously have been college-bound compete instead for trade jobs, they will, of course, end up displacing less academically inclined people who may have been a better fit for those jobs. That will leave even fewer options for a large number of workers.

We see evidence of this trend already in the daily news. Newspapers routinely report that people are specifically seeking jobs that can't be offshored. Much is made of new "green collar jobs that cannot be outsourced." While this is certainly a desirable development, we have to acknowledge that the bulk of these jobs are going to involve installing solar panels, wind turbines and so forth. They are trade jobs; not jobs for college graduates.

The cost to society of such a turn away from education would be enormous. It would damage the hopes, dreams and expectations of our children and potentially rob them of things that we ourselves have come to take for granted. Those workers whose prospects were diminished by a new influx of more "book smart" competitors would become even more dispirited and more likely to turn to crime or other undesirable alternatives. This harsh new reality would fall most heavily on people in disadvantaged sectors of the population. Finally, and perhaps most chillingly, a trend away from college would rob us of talent we may well need in the future.

Econometrics: Looking Backward

The majority of mainstream economists, upon whom we depend to detect and project trends such as the ones we have discussed here, do not seem to be particularly concerned about a potential transition to an automated economy. They hold firm to the belief that the economy will continuously generate jobs within the capabilities of the average worker—and that this process will continue indefinitely. I think the reason that economists cannot see what is really happening may be that they are simply too buried in their data.

In recent decades, the field of economics has been increasingly taken over by the branch of the field known as *econometrics*. Econometrics is essentially a merger of economics and statistics. Econometricians engage in the task of analyzing reams of past economic data. They apply advanced statistical techniques and create complex computer models. In fact, it would be fair to say that econometrics is another example of change that has come about as a result of our vast increase in computational capability. Without computers, there would certainly be far fewer econometricians.

Unfortunately, the purveyors of econometrics labor under the delusion that they are economists, when in fact they are historians. Statistics is well suited to measuring things which are relatively constant or which are changing gradually. It works great for baseball and for projecting demographic trends. It does not, however, do well in an environment that is that is likely to be increasingly impacted by a geometric or exponential change. The graph that follows should help illustrate this point.

Econometrics: Looking Backward

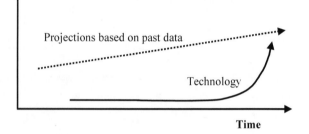

The reasoning of the econometrician is illustrated by the straight, gradually increasing line. He or she assumes that it is possible to crunch data from two, five or even ten years ago and discern trends that will likely hold true in the future. The problem is compounded by the fact that a basic tenet of statistics is the idea that more data gives a more reliable result. For our econometrician, more data often means going even further back into the past. So a study based on ten years worth of data might well be considered better than one looking at only the last two years.

The problem with all this is shown by the other line on this chart. This, of course, is the geometrically increasing line that represents technological advance. Obviously, technology is going to have a highly disruptive impact on the assumptions of the econometricians. Why have they not seen it? Because a geometric advance starts out very gradually and then, very suddenly, begins to increase dramatically. In fact, by the time econometrics shows clear evidence of what is happening, it will be very late in the game. Economists looking at past data are always *looking back* at the flat (left) part of the geometrically increasing technology line. Prior to the point where the impact becomes obvious, there is really no way past data can show them the steep vertical part of the line that lies ahead.

The Luddite Fallacy

As mentioned previously, economists have invented a concept, named in honor of the 1811 Luddite movement, called the *Luddite fallacy*. This line of reasoning says that, while technological progress will cause some workers to lose their jobs as a result of outdated skills, any concern that advancing technology will lead to widespread, increasing unemployment is, in fact, a fallacy. In other words, machine automation will *never* lead to economy-wide, systemic unemployment. The reasoning offered by economists is that, as automation increases the productivity of workers, it leads to lower prices for products and services, and in turn, those lower prices result in increased consumer demand. As businesses strive to meet that increased demand, they ramp up production—and that means new jobs.

Faith in the reasoning behind the Luddite fallacy is deeply ingrained in most professional and academic economists. William Easterly is a professor at New York University and an expert in the economies of developing countries. In his book *The Elusive Quest for Growth: Economists' Adventures and Misadventures in the Tropics,*[1] Easterly very well expresses the conventional view that we set out to challenge when we created our tunnel simulation in Chapter 1. His main point is that, as advancing technology increases productivity, prices will fall, demand will increase, and the economy will therefore produce more goods and services. In other words, the same number of workers will be employed but they will *produce more.*[32]

The question we have to ask is: where will this increase in demand come from? *Who* is going to step forward and purchase all this increased output? As we have seen in this chapter, automation stands poised to fall across the board—on nearly every industry, on a wide range of occupations, and on workers with graduate degrees as well as on those without high school diplomas. Automation will come to the developed nations and to the developing ones. The consumers that drive our markets

---

[1] This is in no way intended to disparage Easterly's book—which gives many very useful insights into the economic issues related to poverty in third world countries. Easterly's book is cited here because it offers a very cohesive explanation of the reasoning accepted by the majority of economists. We should also note that the book primarily deals with developing nations in the tropics. These countries are starting from a low technological level and may well have export-driven economies, and so it is not unreasonable to assume that their economic development would follow the historical trend seen in advanced countries. However, if we extend this idea to include the future broad-based integration of advanced technologies such as robotics and artificial intelligence in to the entire world economy, it falls apart. These technologies are game changers: at some point in the future, they are going to fundamentally alter the relationship between workers and machines.

are virtually all people who either have a job or depend on someone who has a job. When a substantial fraction of these people are no longer employed, where will market demand come from?

The world economy is a closed system; there are no export markets to prop up the world economy in the way that the Southern slave economy was sustained. Nearly every consumer—every light in our tunnel—derives income from a job. If we automate the bulk of those jobs away, demand must fall. No wealthy Martians are going to step up to the plate and buy stuff from us.

Economists' faith that the Luddite fallacy is, well, a fallacy—and indeed in much of generally accepted economic theory—rests on two fundamental assumptions about the relationship between workers and machines: (1) machines are tools which are used by, and increase the productivity of, workers, and (2) the vast majority of workers in our population are capable of becoming machine operators; in other words, the average worker can (with proper training) add value to the tasks performed by machines. What happens when these assumptions fail? What happens when machines *become* workers—when capital becomes labor?

It is important to note that such a change in the relationship between workers and machines will have a *worldwide* impact. Advanced machine automation will come to low wage countries as well as developed nations. A 2003 article in *AutomationWorld* pointed out that "productivity gains spawned by factory automation are driving a worldwide decline in manufacturing jobs, even in developing nations."[33] According to the article, even back in 2003, automation was causing significant job loss in Brazil, India and China.

We cannot succumb to the temptation to assume that the rising middle classes in China and India are going to solve the demand problem. Our simulation in Chapter 1 used *just one* tunnel to represent the entire world mass market. Export and import flows between nations are not simulated in our tunnel because they are just accounting contrivances. Our tunnel is just a bunch of lights—each of which represents someone, somewhere with a job.

The conventional view is echoed strongly by former Federal Reserve Chairman Alan Greenspan in his book, *The Age of Turbulence*. Greenspan's book includes an entire chapter devoted to the growing problem of income inequality. Greenspan tells us that income in the United States is now more concentrated than at any time since the late 1920s.[34] He correctly attributes this to globalization and, especially, technological advance, pointing out that many of the jobs previously held by "moderately skilled workers" are now handled by computers. What Greenspan apparently fails to see is that technological progress *will never stop, and in fact, may well accelerate*. While today jobs that require low and moderately skilled workers are being computerized, tomorrow it will be jobs performed by highly skilled and educated workers. Indeed, this is already happening among information technology professionals, where jobs that once required college degrees are simply vanishing into the computer network.

Greenspan's suggested solution is that we dramatically improve our elementary and secondary education systems. While that is a goal that I certainly support, the idea that it will solve the problem is simply not a realistic expectation. Even if we could wave a magic wand and improve education in the United States overnight, it would obviously be years before those children enter the workforce. In the meantime, computer technology will continue its relentless advance. The subtitle of Chairman Greenspan's book is "Adventures in a New World." However, it appears that, like most economists, he has failed to perceive just how new that world really is.

The reality is that the Luddite fallacy amounts to nothing more than a historical observation. Since things have worked out so far, economists assume that they will always work out. For centuries, machines have continuously become more sophisticated, and as a result, the productivity—and therefore the wages—of the average worker have increased. It stands to reason that if this process continues indefinitely, at some point the machines will become autonomous, and the worker will no longer add value. Long before that extremity is reached, however, there must come a tipping point at which job losses from automation begin to overwhelm any positive impact on employment from lower prices and increased consumer demand. (For more on this, please see pages 131-138 in Chapter 3). In light of unprecedented, geometrically advancing computer technology, the Luddite "fallacy" does not really look all that fallacious.

A More Ambitious View of Future Technological Progress: The Singularity

In this book, I have been quite conservative in terms of projecting where technology may take us. I have spoken of robots that may eventually manage to stock store shelves and of other robots that might be remotely controlled from low wage countries. I have not spoken of armies of marauding, humanoid robots, or of intelligent computers taking control of nuclear weapons. Partly, the reason is that I want to come across as very down to earth. I want you to take this book seriously. A second reason is that none of those science fiction-like scenarios are at all necessary. Technology—if we do not prepare for it—does not need to directly or physically attack us to cause us great harm. The only thing it needs to do is take our jobs.

Nonetheless, I would be remiss if I didn't include the fact that many extremely well regarded individuals with deep experience in science and technology have a far more ambitious view of what is ultimately possible. World-renowned cosmologist and author of the book, *A Brief History of Time*, Stephen Hawking, has said, "Computers are likely to overtake humans in intelligence at some point in the next hundred years."[35] Inventor and author Ray Kurzweil, who received the National Medal of Technology from President Clinton in 1999, is far more optimistic and predicts that machines will achieve true intelligence by 2029.

Kurzweil is also one of the leading proponents of the *technological singularity*, which he expects to occur by the year 2045.[36] This concept, which was originally introduced by the mathematician and author Vernor Vinge,[37] suggests that at some point in the future, technological progress will simply explode incomprehensibly. Basically, things will just get away from us. If you look at the now familiar chart that follows, the technological singularity would occur at some point close to where the line becomes nearly vertical. Beyond this point, it is just straight up.

The Technological Singularity

Many people have postulated that the singularity will be brought on when machines finally become smarter than us, and then apply that higher intelligence to the task of designing even better versions of themselves. After that, human beings would no longer be able to understand the progress taking place.

It seems obvious that if the singularity does indeed take place, nearly all of us could potentially be out of a job. People with PhDs from top universities could well find themselves in the same boat as autoworkers in Detroit. How could the average people who make up the bulk of our population earn a living in a world in which machines were smarter and more capable than even the most intelligent humans?

Aside from the issue of providing essential support for the population, the singularity introduces a more basic economic paradox. In a free market economy, nothing is produced unless there is demand—and "demand" in economic terms means desire combined with the ability to pay. There is no incentive to produce products if there are no consumers with sufficient discretionary income to purchase those products. This is true even if intelligent machines someday become super-efficient producers. If average—or even exceptional—human beings are unable to find employment within their capabilities, then how will they acquire the income necessary to create the demand that in turn drives production? If we consider the singularity in this context, then is it really something that will necessarily push us forward exponentially? Or could it in actuality lead to rapid economic decline?[1]

---

[1] The technologists who speculate about the singularity don't seem too concerned about this problem. Perhaps they assume that the super-intelligent machines of the future will figure all this out for us. However, if something other than consumer demand drives production, then we no longer have a market economy; we will then have a planned economy. The Soviet Union, of course, didn't have intelligent machines—but they did have lots of very intelligent mathematicians staffing an agency called *Gosplan,* which attempted to figure things out. Let's hope the machines will do a better job. (Please see "The Technology Paradox" in the Appendix for more on this.)

In this book, we won't again stray into this more speculative arena (except in the last sections of the Appendix). The ideas presented in this book *do not* depend on the occurrence of the technological singularity. The standard we have set is much lower: we are concerned only with the possibility that machines will become capable of performing most average, routine jobs. The singularity represents a far more extreme case. It's fair to say, however, that if something along the lines of the technological singularity is to occur, we may first need a paradigm shift in the way our economy works—or at least some changes in our economic architecture. Otherwise, we will be in for quite a shock.

A War on Technology

In this chapter we have seen that computers are increasing in both power and number at a simply astonishing rate. We've looked at clear evidence that shows we have essentially hit the ceiling in terms of what we can expect from future increases in the capability of average human beings. We've also looked at a variety of specific job types and technologies and shown how automation is likely to have a much broader impact than many of us might imagine— and also how the jobs of many highly paid and highly educated workers may be among the most vulnerable. Let's look again at the assumption we set out to test at the beginning of this chapter:

Technology will not advance to the point where the bulk of jobs performed by typical people will be automated before the year 2089.

Prior to that year, the economy will always create jobs that are within the capabilities of the vast majority of the human population.

At this point, it seems very difficult to support this assumption. Most of the trends we have reviewed in this chapter are likely to come into play *long before* our cutoff date of 2089. It is very possible that even advanced nanotechnology would be available within that time frame. We therefore cannot escape the conclusion that we will very likely have to deal with the impact of across-the-board automation in our lifetimes, or at the very least, within the lifetimes of our children.

If we do not have a strategy—and specific policies—in place to deal with this issue before its full impact arrives, the outcome will be decidedly negative. As the trend toward systemic job loss increases, it is quite easy to foresee a number of possible ramifications. I have already mentioned the likelihood of a drop in college enrollment and a migration toward safer trade jobs. Another trend that will surely occur as recognition sets in will be a general "war on technology." Workers in virtually every occupation—even many of those who themselves work in technical fields—will desperately, and quite understandably, attempt to protect their livelihoods.

We can expect substantial pressure on government to somehow restrict technological progress and job automation. It is possible that there will be a significant, last-ditch resurgence in the power of organized labor. Workers in jobs and industries that are not now organized will very possibly turn to unions in an attempt to exert some power over their own futures. The result is likely to be somewhat slowed technical progress, work stoppages, and significant economic and social disruptions.

The economists who believe in the premise of the Luddite fallacy are *not* wrong about one thing: technological advancement is the *only* thing that can, over the long term, drive us toward continuing economic growth. Continuing technical progress is our only hope for a wealthier society in the future.

We know that in the coming decades, we will face enormous new challenges. Most notable will be the related issues of increasing energy scarcity and climate change. We are likely to face a wide-ranging impact on climate, agriculture and even geography—including the possibility of rising ocean levels that could result in humanitarian disasters of unimaginable proportions. As we are all aware, currently the efforts to mitigate global warming and the other important environmental impacts from burning fossil fuels are enjoying very limited success. The unfortunate reality is that we may ultimately be forced to accept the fact that we will fail—at least to some degree—in our quest to stop climate change. But the costs associated with somehow adapting to those changes will be astronomical. At the same time, reserves of oil, natural gas, and in the longer run even coal, are going to be depleted. How can we hope to face these challenges if our economy is in decline and the bulk of our population is focused almost exclusively on the continuity of individual incomes?

A similar point can be made regarding the global war on poverty. How can we hope to win this war, if we ourselves are not prosperous? We know that poverty is one of the primary drivers of war, conflict and terrorism. In a long-term stagnant or declining economic environment, these problems will only grow.

The answer cannot be to attempt to halt technological progress. The problem is not with technology; it is with our economic system, and it lies specifically in that system's inability to continue thriving in the new reality that is being created. It will be extraordinarily difficult to make material changes to that system because it has served us so well, for so long. Nonetheless, in the final chapters of this book, I will suggest some changes that I believe will allow us to move from fearing technology to leveraging it as never before and then deploying it against the challenges we will face. Before then, however, we must move from our tunnel simulation back into the real world. There we will see that the situation is probably far more dangerous and perhaps more immediate than we have yet imagined.

Chapter 3

DANGER

In the first chapter of this book, our tunnel simulation showed that, as large numbers of workers were automated out of their jobs, the economy would eventually go into decline because each worker is also a consumer (and may support other consumers) in the mass market. In the real world, it seems very likely that the automation process would be a fairly gradual one. Can we assume, therefore, that the economic impact of this transition would also be gradual in nature and might not be apparent until some point in the distant future? To answer this question, let's look at how markets work in the real world.

The Predictive Nature of Markets

One of the more interesting developments to arise out of the Internet has been the appearance of online prediction markets. A prediction market is really just another name for a betting market, and it operates in a similar fashion to the futures markets that allow traders to place bets on the future direction of things like oil prices and stock market indexes. Prediction markets, such as the Iowa Electronic Markets (IEM) and Intrade, allow participants to bet real money on things like elections, economic developments (such as recessions), or specific events in the business or entertainment worlds.

While prediction markets are specifically set up to predict future events, we know that we can expand this idea and say that all free markets are, in essence, prediction markets. If you buy a particular company's stock, then you are placing a bet that, in the future, that stock will trade at a higher value. Collectively, the millions of participants in the world's stock markets often act as a sort of predictive barometer for the economy as a whole. Historically, the U.S. stock market has often anticipated recessions by six months or so. Likewise, recovery from a recession is very often preceded by a rise in the stock market.

This predictive feature also applies to all the other various markets with which we interact, including the housing market, the job market, and the mass market for goods and services. The reason is quite obvious. People are rational beings and every individual, to some degree, incorporates his or her expectations for the future into his or her current actions. If you expect that you will receive a large sum of money at some point in the near future, you are very likely to begin spending some of that money even before you actually receive it.

Now we can begin to see a potential problem. As automation begins to eliminate jobs in an increasingly wide range of industries and occupations, its impacts are clearly not going to be kept a secret. People will become aware of what is happening—even if it is not officially recognized by governments—and they will begin to modify their current behavior accordingly. As a growing percentage of the population is exposed to direct evidence of ongoing job losses, many people will begin to experience a greatly heightened level of stress and worry. Facing this, individuals will take the obvious action: they will cut back on consumption, perhaps quite dramatically, and try to save more in anticipation of a very uncertain future.

It is important to note that what we are talking about here is really not the same as what occurs in the normal business cycle. In a typical recession, many consumers will also cut back on spending as they worry about losing their jobs, and this will tend to deepen the downturn. However, this worry is predominantly a short-term concern because people realize that, in the long run, when the economy recovers, businesses will have to again begin hiring.

But what if, at some point in the coming decades, there is a general coalescence of belief that suggests the basic character of the economy has changed to such an extent that jobs may *not* be available—or at least will be very hard to obtain—in the future? If this were to occur in a critical mass of the consumers who participate in the market, in the absence of an effective government policy, we could clearly be thrust into a very dark scenario. An individual faced with possible long-term or even permanent unemployment at some point in the foreseeable future is in essence looking at an involuntary, early and unpredictable retirement. Seeing this, consumers might begin to adjust their current consumption in light of such extreme uncertainty. If this were to occur, a dramatic economic downward spiral would almost certainly be precipitated.

If such a disastrous event were to occur, the standard responses employed by governments, such as stimulus spending, would probably be largely ineffective. This is because stimulus spending (or tax cuts) would not address people's long-term concern about their incomes; it seems very likely that any additional income received by consumers would immediately be saved. It is, in fact, very difficult to imagine a government policy short of somehow guaranteeing individuals' continuity of income that would be effective in such a scenario. And undertaking such an income guarantee policy in the midst of such a severe economic downturn would be extraordinarily difficult and expensive. In short, the consequences of such a scenario are really not something we would want to contemplate.

The 2008-2009 Recession

Obviously, our current economy remains highly dependent on the efforts of human workers. We can probably, therefore, assume that the dangerous scenario described above lies in the fairly distant future—perhaps even decades from now. Nonetheless, I think we can expect that, long before we reach such an extreme point, the economy will begin to display evidence of the overall impact of automation. Is it possible that, at least to some extent, this has been a factor in the current crisis? As we all know, the 2008-9 recession began with the 2007 subprime meltdown that then evolved into the credit crunch and global financial crisis. As I pointed out in Chapter 2, advancing computer technology certainly played an enabling role in the severity and global nature of the current situation. Beyond this, there are a number of other factors that should concern us as we look forward to recovery from the current recession.

The freeze-up of credit in 2008 struck an especially hard blow at consumer demand because, over the last eight years or so, real wages for most average Americans have been stagnant or even declining while health care costs have been exploding. Faced with this, many consumers turned to home equity loans and credit cards in order to maintain their standard of living. The collapse of these credit lines in 2008, together with rapidly rising unemployment, forced consumers to cut back in a fairly dramatic way. Automation, offshore factory relocations and, to a lesser extent service job offshoring, have certainly played an important role in this trend toward declining or stagnant wages.

Globalization, and in particular the need for American manufacturers to compete against low cost producers in China, has forced job cuts and accelerated the drive toward automation. This has been reflected in the substantial productivity increases of the U.S. economy in recent years. While the impact of globalization on the job market has received most of the attention, I think most economists would be likely to agree that advancing technology and job automation have played a far more significant role.

Although factors such as stagnating wages for average workers would seem to provide support for the theory that automation is beginning to have a significant impact on the economy's ability to create jobs, it is important to note that there are also signals which tend to contradict this conclusion: before the advent of the current crisis, unemployment as measured by the government, remained very low. However, there is also evidence that *underemployment*, especially cases where workers have been forced to settle for one or more part time jobs rather than a full time position, has been a significant issue for some time. In short, the evidence is not conclusive; but I think there may well be reasonable cause for concern.

I don't think it would be unreasonable to say that among many average workers, there is now a sense that good jobs are more difficult to find and keep than in the past. The term "jobless recovery" is now routinely applied to nearly every post-recession economic recovery, and there is no reason to expect that the current case will be an exception. One reason is likely that, when bottom lines are pressured during a downturn, businesses have an even bigger incentive to turn toward job eliminating technologies. In many cases, as efficiency continues to increase even during a downturn, businesses find that they are able to avoid rehiring displaced workers once a recovery develops.

If, in fact, automation is beginning to have an increasingly significant impact, I think there is a very real concern that, even with the unprecedented level of stimulus spending that has been pursued, the number of jobs ultimately created may turn out to be disappointing. Without specific policies and incentives in place to help ensure job creation, much of the stimulus may leak away—much like heat escaping from a poorly insulated house. In particular, a great deal of the indirect economic stimulus created by government spending is likely to end up being directed overseas and to capital rather than to labor. Later in this chapter I will propose some specific policy initiatives that I feel would greatly assist in job creation.

Offshoring and Factory Migration

In Chapter 2 we saw that offshoring is often really just the leading edge of automation. When a job is offshored, a new consumer is created in a developing nation—at least temporarily. However, from the point of view of consumers in the United States or Western Europe, offshoring looks exactly the same as automation. The same can be said of relocating a factory to a developing country like China; to workers in the U.S. it looks exactly the same as simply building a fully automated factory. In other words, service offshoring and factory relocations accelerate the job loss as well as the psychological impact on workers (consumers) and make it likely that the dangerous scenario described above could occur even earlier in the developed nations. And it is these developed economies that remain the primary consumption drivers of the world economy as a whole.

In essence, we have succeeded in globalizing labor and capital, but we have really *not* globalized consumption. To a large extent, workers in low wage countries are not capable of purchasing the goods they are producing. Or even if they can afford to buy those products, they are unlikely to do so because they are much more interested in saving. Consumers in the United States are expected to continue powering the factories in China and other developing nations even as the jobs from which those consumers derive their income evaporate.' This is clearly unsustainable.

This danger—together with the fact that the benefits from offshoring in the third world are likely to be only transitory since automation will follow—really calls into question the overall wisdom of this practice. This is true even for the developing nations that are currently benefiting from offshoring because, as we will see later, the consequences of such a severe and long lasting economic downturn in the West would almost certainly wipe out and reverse any temporary gains these countries may have obtained from offshoring.

Of course, the overall wisdom of a practice like offshoring has absolutely no bearing on the actions of individual businesses. Businesses act according to short-term incentives and the competition that they face. Even a CEO who dislikes offshoring will have little choice but to pursue the practice if his or her competitors choose to do so. Only governments have the ability to create incentives and policies that can potentially turn things around and avoid the disastrous economic spiral that might occur if a

---

' Many economists would argue that this is not a major concern because the U.S. economy will evolve so that most consumers derive their income from jobs in the service sector, and that these services will be provided *locally*. However, as we have seen in this book, many local services will also ultimately be subject to both offshoring and automation.

critical mass of consumers someday lose confidence in the future job market.

Reconsidering Conventional Views about the Future

Pick up any recently published book which attempts to forecast the major trends likely to develop in the coming decades, and you will quickly come to the conclusion that there is a very conventional set of views on where we are headed. Many of these widely held beliefs about the future are based on simple, and inescapable, demographic analysis—and, in particular, on *counting workers.* What will be most important in the future? The conventional answer is: first, the number of workers as compared with the number of retired persons in most countries, and second the number of workers (and the wages they are willing to accept) in developing nations like China as compared with the number of workers in advanced countries.

Two of the most notable books that have fleshed out these commonly held views are *The World is Flat: A Brief History of the Twenty-first Century* by Thomas Friedman and *Futurecast: how superpowers, populations, and globalization will change the way you live and work* by Robert J. Shapiro. In his book, Shapiro gives a very insightful analysis of the conventional view.[38] He identifies three basic forces that he feels will shape the coming decades: (1) The demographic crisis—or "baby boom" problem—that will result in most countries having an unprecedented number of elderly persons relative to the number of workers in their populations. (2) Globalization, which allows labor and capital, as well as products and many services to move effortlessly across borders, and (3) The fall of Soviet-style communism and the adoption of market-based economies throughout the world. This has resulted in hundreds of millions of workers who were previously locked away in centrally planned economies now being free to enter the global workforce.

The first thing you might notice is that the issue we have been focusing on in this book—technological acceleration—does not appear in the list at all. In fact, in the conventional view of the future, technology is primarily seen as an enabler of globalization. It has been relegated to a secondary, supporting role. Somehow, technology has faded into the background. Nearly everyone agrees that technology has played an important role in making globalization possible, and that globalization is certainly a highly disruptive force, but now everyone seems to expect that technology will be put back into its box. It will behave. Technology's role will be to continue pushing the existing trends forward so that the projection lines all the analysts have drawn will remain nice and straight.

Friedman's book, *The World is Flat*, offers a longer list of ten forces that have "flattened" the world, and he does include some facets of technology in that list.[39] However, the focus is almost entirely on specific technologies that enable global competition and collaboration. No attention is given to the overall impact of accelerating technology, and in particular, subjects such as artificial intelligence and robotics go virtually unmentioned. I suspect that this will prove to be a remarkable oversight in a book that is subtitled "A Brief History of the Twenty-first Century."

Shapiro correctly notes that there is an increasing trend toward breaking jobs up into pieces and then offshoring these individual tasks and that this trend has been enabled by the availability of new productivity software that makes it possible for workers in developing countries to perform increasingly complex tasks. All this is undoubtedly true. However, the real question is this: if software can be developed that enables low wage workers to do all these things, then why would this technology just arbitrarily stop there? Clearly, it would not. It will continue advancing to the point where *no person at all is required*—and it may well do so in far less time than we might expect.

The reality is that nearly everyone who attempts to forecast the coming decades seems to identify the wrong trend. Those who subscribe to the conventional view fail to see that untold millions of competing and collaborating global workers are ultimately likely to be flattened by the major force that will truly shape the new century. Globalization is certainly significant, but it is really a mere offshoot of the primary force driving us toward change, and that force continues to be technology.

The China Fallacy

No conventional view is more widely held than the belief that the future is likely to belong to China. Once again, this projection is based primarily on demographics. I have seen studies where researchers project as far out as 2050—more than 40 years into the future. To do this, analysts take a per-capita income that is somewhat comparable to that of developed nations and then multiply it by some huge fraction of the Chinese population. In other words, they assume that a very significant percentage of the 1.3 billion people in China are going to be dragged into the middle class. And, the primary force that will do that dragging is going to be the ever-expanding employment of hundreds of millions of workers in China's manufacturing sector.

Currently, a large percentage of Chinese manufacturing is focused on simple, very low value products. Plastic ornaments and toys for Christmas and Halloween come to mind. Increasingly, however, Chinese manufacturing is expected to creep up the value chain. More complex products will be produced. It's generally assumed that Chinese companies will become a disruptive force in the global automotive market at some point in the not too distant future.

For all this, automation will be essential. The large industrial corporations in the United States, Germany and Japan that provide this automation technology are certainly salivating at the prospect of the future market that China will provide. The Chinese government, meanwhile, is focused on insuring that as much of this technology as possible gets transferred to native businesses. Automation is not just about saving money by eliminating jobs. Automation conveys benefits far beyond that: it makes more precise and reliable manufacturing possible. Machines can

---

[1] Those who disagree with my argument here will likely cite anecdotal evidence of Chinese companies that have so far succeeded by substi-

simply do things better, faster and with more precision than can any human worker—regardless of the prevailing wage level. In the future, mass market products are likely to become more sophisticated, and in many cases physically smaller. Tolerances will be tighter and the need for precision greater. Automation is going to fall heavily on China's manufacturing sector and, in the long run, the impact on employment is likely to be dramatic.

Another potential problem that China seems likely to face is stagnant or declining demand for its exports in the United States and other developed nations. As we have seen, as jobs are lost in the Western countries and fear of structural unemployment there grows, consumer demand will fall. The reality is that China does not have an integrated, self-sustaining economy. A substantial fraction of its factories are geared toward exports, and these exports are largely responsible for the phenomenal economic growth that China has enjoyed in recent years.

Evidence of this is clearly seen in the stalling growth that is resulting from the 2008-9 recession. As of early 2009, thousands of Chinese factories have shut down and millions of workers have lost their jobs. The Xinhua news

---

tuting low cost labor for automation. BYD, a manufacturer of batteries and automobiles is one example. The question is whether that business model is sustainable. I would argue that, especially in the automotive market, the company will ultimately have to introduce more automation to meet the quality standards required in export markets. It's also worth noting that such a business model could be sustained in the long run only if wages in China remain extremely low indefinitely. If that is the case, how will China succeed in driving domestic consumption and achieving a more balanced economy which is less dependent on exports?

agency reported that in January 2009 that Chinese Premier Wen Jiabao told the state council that 2009 would be the "most difficult year for China's economic development so far this century." Aside from exports, the major factor propping up the Chinese economy is the continuing enormous investment in infrastructure. Clearly however, this level of spending is not sustainable indefinitely.

Many analysts have called for China to stimulate its domestic demand in order to help make up for this decline in demand for exports. In reality, this will be very difficult. The majority of the products produced in Chinese factories are either not affordable to Chinese consumers, or they are of no interest. Chinese people are not going to buy those Halloween trinkets. Even if production could be redirected to domestic needs, demand would still not materialize because of China's extraordinarily high savings rate.

The percentage of income saved by workers in China has been estimated to be as high as 30 percent. This compares with a saving rate in the United States that—at least up until the start of the current economic crisis—has been essentially zero. Several reasons can be given for this high savings rate. A number of economists point to the fact that China has no social safety nets such as retirement pensions, unemployment insurance or health care insurance for the vast majority of its population. Others[40] argue that the high saving rate is due to intentional government policies that repress consumer spending. It is very likely that both of these factors play a significant role, but my personal opinion is that the importance of saving for the future is simply integrated deeply into Chinese culture. Obviously, something like that is very hard to turn around. It seems extraordinarily unlikely that any government policy would succeed in substantially increasing Chinese consumer spending—especially in a time of general economic distress.

Even if we put aside the issue of automation, the immense size of China's population relative to the global economy represents a significant challenge to its long-term development. As smaller countries such as Japan and South Korea industrialized, wages in those countries inevitably rose, and their populations were largely elevated into a consumer class. China, however, is so large that the number of available workers is seemingly limitless.

In addition, the government actively enforces discrimination that tends to drive wages even lower. Much of the work in China's factories is performed by migrant workers who officially live in the countryside but are allowed to come to cities or industrial regions to work. These workers typically live in factory dormitories and do not have the right to bring their families to the cities or to genuinely assimilate into an urban middle class. Wages for these workers are far lower than for urban dwellers, and the money that they do earn is for the most part either saved or sent home to help support their families. These workers are not in a position to become major drivers of local consumption any time soon.

My own opinion on the future of China may well be dismissed as being too pessimistic. I do not believe that China can fully industrialize along the same path followed in the West. China is too late—and simply too big. China's economic development, for all of its phenomenal progress, is in a race with technology, and that is a race it cannot win.

If I am even partly correct in this projection, then the ramifications for the rest of the world will be enormous. In the West, we look to the impending economic might of China with mixed emotions. On the one hand, we worry about all that power residing in a country that may well continue to be essentially undemocratic for the foreseeable future. On the other hand, many of our hopes for the future are tied directly to the assumption that unfettered economic growth will continue in China. We look forward to enormous new markets for our products and services, and we have even gone so far as to pin our hopes for a resolution to some of our own demographic problems to our expectations for China.

Most people are aware that as the population ages in Western countries, a tremendous amount of pressure will be put on pension programs like Social Security in the United States and on retiree health programs. What is less often discussed is that there is also a potential problem with the general value of assets. As people work throughout their careers they save for retirement. The majority of this goes into stocks and bonds, often via 401(k) plans. When these people then reach retirement age, they begin to sell those assets in order to maintain their standard of living.

The problem is that, for the first time, we will have a very large number of older people actively selling assets, while at the same time, a relatively smaller number of younger workers will be available to buy those assets. The obvious result is that asset values of nearly all types are likely to fall under the duress of this lopsided selling pressure. A number of people—including Alan Greenspan in his book *The Age of Turbulence*—have suggested that the solution to this problem is going to be huge numbers of newly wealthy young workers from China, India and other developing nations who will step forward to buy our assets. As we have seen, that might not be such a good bet.

The reality is that the idea of this tremendous new market resulting from an exploding Chinese middle class is something of a mirage. The Chinese middle class is not an independent market. These people are essentially standing on the shoulders of American and European consumers. And as we have noted again and again in this book, those Western consumers all depend on jobs. If automation begins to dramatically impact employment in China, while at the same time demand dwindles in the West—and certainly if the catastrophic event described at the beginning of this chapter occurs—then this economic perpetual motion machine is going to collapse.

Given all this, what can we really say about the future of China? Nearly a fourth of the world's population lives in China; therefore, there is no doubt that this country will continue to have significant, and perhaps increasing, influence in the decades to come. However, simply extrapolating current trends is very unlikely to give an accurate projection. China is going to be heavily impacted by accelerating technology, and its future—along with the future of developed nations—is going to be highly unpredictable. Its fate will ultimately be determined by the Chinese government's ability to maintain control and civil order and to adapt to the changes that are coming.

In terms of economics, the most important challenge for China is likely to be transitioning to a self-sustaining economy that is driven by internal consumption rather than by exports. As we have seen, this will be very difficult because of low wages, a growing unemployment problem and the Chinese propensity to save rather than consume. However, local consumption will be increasingly essential because the primary incentives which drive the private sector to locate manufacturing in countries like China are likely to shift dramatically in the coming decades.

The Future of Manufacturing

Recent years have seen a mass migration of manufacturing to developing countries. Low labor costs have clearly been the primary incentive underlying this trend. In the future, however, factories of all types are likely to become increasingly automated. As the years and decades progress, labor costs will comprise a smaller and smaller component of manufacturers' cost structures.

To get some insight into how automation is likely to continue impacting manufacturing, it may help to look at a sector which has already been heavily automated: agriculture in the United States. In her book *Travels of a T-shirt in the Global Economy*, economist Pietra Rivoli tells the story of cotton farming in West Texas. Up until the 1920s, every aspect of cotton farming was highly labor intensive. Fields were ploughed with mules, and once the crop was planted, a constant backbreaking vigil was required in order to keep the weeds at bay. Harvesting required the availability of large numbers of workers at precisely the right time— before unfavorable weather conditions destroyed or reduced the value of the crop.

Over the decades, however, the process has become increasingly mechanized. Today cotton farming in West Texas is almost literally a "one-man show."[41] A single farmer with access to tractors, specialized machinery and chemical herbicides can now function almost entirely alone. No workers are required, and the labor content of cotton produced in West Texas is essentially zero.

Obviously, not every agricultural sector is as automated as cotton farming, but there can be absolutely no doubt that the mechanization of agriculture in developed nations has resulted in a massive and irreversible elimination of jobs. The reality is that the manufacturing sector is following the same path. In her book, Rivoli also cites evidence showing that many of the jobs lost in the U.S. textile industry are in fact due to machine automation rather than globalization, and that China, in spite of its low wage

---

Cotton farming in poor countries, of course, remains highly labor intensive. However, this should not be used to argue that manufacturing in poor countries will also remain unchanged. The dynamics of these sectors are very different—poor farmers are subject to many factors which keep mechanization at bay, including lack of education and access to capital, small plots with poor economy of scale, trade barriers, and often outright exploitation at the hands of governments and corrupt officials. Manufacturing in China is very different from agriculture in Africa (or even China).

workforce, lost nearly two million textile jobs to improving automation technology between 1995 and 2002.[42]

It is easy to imagine factories of the future that are almost entirely automated and run by a few skilled technicians. As labor costs fall, we can expect that energy costs will be rising. Nearly all analysts agree that world oil production will peak at some point in the coming years and decades. Beyond this point, in the absence of replacement energy technologies, the cost of fossil fuels is likely to rise inexorably. Given this, we can reasonably expect that the primary incentives for locating the factories of the future will shift away from seeking low labor costs and toward minimizing energy costs.

One of the most significant drivers of energy expenditure is, of course, transportation. Economists Jeff Rubin and Benjamin Tal have suggested that soaring transportation costs resulting from high energy prices alone may be sufficient to reverse globalization. They point out that once oil reaches a price of $150/barrel, the additional transportation costs are essentially equivalent to the tariffs that existed in the 1970s.[43]

In a world with automated factories and high energy costs, there will be clear incentives toward distributed manufacturing. It will make sense to locate factories as close as possible to consumers and/or to the natural resources used as inputs in the production process. A primary motivation in locating factories will be to minimize the transportation costs associated with moving both inputs and final products. It is also possible that advancing automation technology may ultimately transform the traditional economy of scale model so that much smaller and more flexible factories located in direct proximity to markets make sense.

Aside from energy costs, a second crucial consideration will be political stability. The forces unleashed by accelerating technology are likely to have a highly disruptive impact on governments throughout the world. Businesses will place increasing importance on minimizing investment risk: they will seek to build factories and hold capital in countries they perceive as stable. In the future, those nations which can adapt to change so as to continue to support sustained consumption, maintain stability and rule of law, and provide reliable access to energy, as well as efficient, energy-minimizing transportation systems, are likely to have a significant competitive advantage in terms of attracting and retaining investment.

India and Offshoring

We've noted that China does not yet have an integrated, self-sustaining modern economy. This is equally true of India. India is essentially an impoverished, developing nation with a government that is democratic, but also often mired in bureaucracy. In the midst of this, India has an isolated island of enormous growth and prosperity: its software and offshoring industries.

India will face exactly the same two retarding forces that are going to hold back China: First, automation is going to invade its offshoring businesses (as well as its traditional industries) and take back many of those jobs. We are likely to see "jobless repatriation" as technology advances to the point where many lower-skill jobs can be performed by computer technology.

Indian companies will probably respond by trying to outrun automation. They will seek to increasingly capture higher value jobs performed by highly educated and paid workers in Western countries. As we have seen, however, even many high skill jobs will ultimately be subject to automation. And any success in capturing higher value jobs will only exacerbate the second problem, which will be the collapse in demand that results from fear of job loss in the West.

Economic and National Security Implications for the United States

What would all this mean for the United States? The answer to that depends entirely on how well the U.S. can adapt to the new reality. The conventional views all point to a decline in global influence and power for the United States. The catch phrases for the coming decades will be "the post-American era" and "the end of American exceptionalism."

Once again, though, those conventional views are all based largely on demographics—on *counting workers*. America is expected to decline because countries like China and India have dramatically more workers—and they are willing to work for less. What if, in the future, workers are not going to be as important as we imagine? What if machines advance to the point where workers become increasingly superfluous to the production process? In that scenario, it is all about who controls technology. And as of the moment, that continues to largely be the United States.

In that sense, the future for the U.S. could potentially be much brighter than the conventional wisdom suggests. But that is only if we can adapt, and that will be a very serious challenge. The United States is fundamentally a conservative country. The risk is very high that we will continue to cling to our existing system simply because it has always worked in the past. If that happens, a great opportunity will be lost, and other countries may well seize the initiative.

If that opportunity is indeed lost, it will clearly have dire national security and military implications for the United States. The obvious reality is that America's military power is entirely dependent on its economic vitality. If the trends projected here are allowed to impact the U.S. economy in an uncontrolled fashion, the likely result will be greatly diminished economic growth (or even sustained decline) and widespread unemployment and social problems. This will clearly detract from the resources and attention that can be allocated to national security.

In the previous chapter, I suggested that there may also be a trend away from college education and toward trade jobs that are perceived as being safer from automation and offshoring. This impact may fall especially heavily on technical fields such as information technology and computer engineering because jobs in these areas are perceived as being especially susceptible to offshoring. Clearly, this will threaten the United States' future leadership position in technology—and therefore its long-term national security.

As we saw previously, the Pentagon envisions a future in which technologies such as robotics and artificial intelligence are deployed increasingly on the battlefield. The reality is that it is impossible to say exactly which technologies will have important military and national security applications in the future. The general acceleration of computer information technology is certain to have a disruptive impact with highly unpredictable results. We can expect that future technologies that emerge in commercial settings will rapidly be redirected into the military arena. It is crucial, therefore, that the U.S. remains competitive in virtually all areas of technology development.

While advancing technology seems likely to ultimately eliminate job opportunities for a large number of average people, maintaining control of that technology will require that the minority of individuals with the capability to make significant contributions to technical fields continue to be educated and trained. These people come from a variety of backgrounds throughout society, and therefore, the disintegration of broad-based incentives to pursue a college education—especially in scientific and technical fields—is likely to be disastrous for the United States in the long run.

Solutions

Now that we've identified the danger we might face and some of the possible implications for the future, let's start thinking about some possible solutions. What could we do to avoid the scary economic scenario we discussed at the beginning of this chapter? In order to answer that, let's start by looking at the idea of labor and capital intensive industries.

Labor and Capital Intensive Industries: The Tipping Point

We can place any industry somewhere on the spectrum that runs from being extremely labor intensive to being highly capital intensive. In our current economy, some of the most labor intensive industries are in the retail, hospitality and small business sectors. Supermarkets, retail chain stores, restaurants and hotels all have to hire lots of workers. Capital intensive industries, on the other hand, hire relatively few workers and instead require investment in technology: in advanced machinery and equipment and in computerized systems. High tech industries such as semiconductor manufacturing, biotechnology and Internet-based companies are all capital intensive.

Over time, as technology advances, most industries become more capital intensive and less labor intensive. Technology also creates entirely new industries, and these are nearly always capital intensive.' This has been going on for centuries, and historically, it has been a good thing. If you compare the industries in a developed nation like the United States with the industries in a third-world nation, you will invariably find that the U.S. economy is far more capital intensive. It has been the introduction of advanced technology that has increased productivity and made the advanced nations of the world rich.

The reason for this goes back to the economists' explanation for the "Luddite fallacy" which we discussed in the previous chapter. As new technology is adopted by industries, production becomes more efficient. This results in some loss of jobs, but it also results in lower prices for goods and services. In other words, it puts more money in consumers' pockets. These consumers then go out and buy all kinds of things, and so the result is increased demand for the products produced by all types of industries. Some of these industries are very labor intensive, so as they strive to meet this increased demand, they are forced to hire more workers. And so, overall employment remains stable or even increases. Sometimes, of course, this results in an unpleasant transition for some workers: they may lose a high paying manufacturing job and end up with a lower paying retail job.

' Consider the case of YouTube, which was acquired by Google for about $1.65 billion in 2006. At the time it was acquired, YouTube had only about 60 employees. That's a valuation of over $27 million per employee. Compare that with about $100,000 per employee for Wal-Mart.

Labor v. Capital Intensive Industries[44]

Company	Employees	Revenue per Employee
McDonalds	400,000	$59,000
Wal-Mart	2,100,000	$180,000
Intel	83,000	$456,000
Microsoft	91,000	$664,000
Google	20,000	$1,081,000

Can this process continue forever? As we saw in the previous chapter, automation technology is likely to increasingly invade the remaining labor intensive sectors of the economy. When this happens, what industries will be left to absorb all the dislocated workers? Look at the table above. What happens when McDonalds begins to look more like Google?

A simple application of common sense should show us that there is some threshold beyond which the overall economy will become *too capital intensive*. Once this happens, lower prices resulting from improved technology will no longer result in increased employment. Beyond this threshold or tipping point, the industries that make up our economy will no longer be forced to hire enough new workers to make up for the job losses resulting from automation; they will instead be able to meet any increase in demand primarily by investing in more technology. As we saw in Chapter 2, this point marks the downfall of economists' faith in the Luddite fallacy, and it also marks the beginning of a downward economic spiral for the simple reason that workers are also the consumers of everything produced in our economy.

What might we expect to happen if the overall economy were approaching this tipping point, beyond which industries would no longer be labor intensive enough to absorb workers who lost their jobs to automation? We would probably expect to see gradually rising unemployment, stagnating wages and significant increases in productivity (output per hour of labor) as industries were able to produce more goods and services with fewer workers.

That sounds uncomfortably close to what actually occurred in the years leading up to the current recession.[ ] In August, 2003, *The Economist* wrote that "the Bureau of Labour Statistics offered the latest evidence of America's productivity revival: output per worker soared by 5.7% in the second quarter, at an annualised rate. But in today's less exuberant times, the figure has raised the unhappy prospect of growth without job creation."[45] Three years later, in an article entitled "The Case of the Missing Jobs," *BusinessWeek* said: "Since 2001, with the aid of computers, telecommunications advances, and ever more efficient plant operations, U.S. manufacturing productivity, or the amount of goods or services a worker produces in an hour, has soared a dizzying 24%....In short: We're making more stuff with fewer people."[46] There is no way to know for sure how close the economy might be to the point

---

[ ] As I noted earlier, we did *not* see an increasing unemployment rate in the years leading up to the current crisis. We did, however, see stagnating wages, increasing productivity and some evidence of underemployment.

where overall job creation will permanently stall. However, these statistics are certainly cause for concern.

The Average Worker and the Average Machine

Another way to express this idea of a tipping point is to think of an average worker using an average machine somewhere in the economy. Obviously, in the real world there are millions of workers using millions of different machines. Over time, of course, those machines have gotten far more sophisticated. Imagine a typical machine that is generally representative of all machines in the economy. At one time, that machine might have been a water wheel driving a mill. Then it became something driven by a steam engine. Later, an industrial machine powered by electricity. Today, the machine is probably controlled by a computer or by embedded microprocessors.

As the average machine has gotten more sophisticated, the wages of the worker operating that machine have increased.[*] As I pointed out in the previous section, more sophisticated machines also make production more efficient and that results in lower prices and, therefore, more money left in consumers' pockets. Consumers then go out and spend that extra money, and that creates jobs for more workers who are likewise operating machines that keep getting better.

---

[*] The idea that long-term economic growth is, to a large extent, the result of advancing technology was formalized by economist Robert Solow in 1956. Economists have lots of different theories about how long-term growth and prosperity come about, but nearly all of them agree that technological progress plays a significant role.

Again, the question we have to ask is: Can this process continue *forever*? I think the answer is no, and the very unpleasant graph on the next page illustrates this.

Value Added (Wage) of Average Worker Operating Average Machine

Also: Overall Wealth of Society (GDP per capita will look similar)

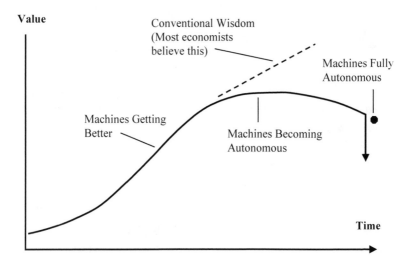

The problem, of course, is that machines are going to get more autonomous. You can see this in the graph at the point where the dotted line (conventional wisdom) and the solid line diverge. As more machines begin to run themselves, the value that the average worker adds begins to decline. Remember that we are talking here about average workers. To get the graph above, you might take the distribution of incomes in the United States and then eliminate both the richest and the poorest people. Then graph the average income of the remaining "typical" people (the bulk of consumers) over time. If you were to instead graph Gross Domestic Product (GDP) per capita, you would end up with a similar graph, but the divergence between the dotted and the solid lines would occur somewhat later. This is because the wealthiest people (who own the machines or have high skill levels) would initially benefit from automation and would drag up the average. Recall that we saw this in our tunnel simulation in Chapter 1.

Once the lines diverge, things get very ugly. This is because the basic mechanism that gets purchasing power into the hands of consumers is breaking down. Eventually, unemployment, low wages—and perhaps most importantly—consumer psychology will cause a very severe downturn. As the graph shows, within the context of our current economic rules, the idea of machines being "fully autonomous" is just a theoretical point that could never actually be reached.

Some people might feel that I am being overly simplistic in equating "technological progress" with "machines getting better." After all, technology is not just physical machines; it is also techniques, processes and distributed knowledge. The reality, however, is that the historical distinction between machines and intellectual capital is blurring. It is now very difficult to separate innovative processes from the advancing information technology that nearly always enables and underlies them. Improved inventory management systems and database marketing are examples of innovative techniques, but they rely heavily on computers. In fact, we can conceivably think of nearly any process or technique as "software"—and, therefore, part of a machine.

If you still have trouble accepting this scenario, you might try asking yourself a couple of questions: (1) Is it possible for a machine to keep getting better *forever* without eventually becoming autonomous? (2) Even if it is possible, then wouldn't the machine someday become so sophisticated that its operation would be beyond the ability of the vast majority of average people? And wouldn't that lead right back to making the machine autonomous?

Capital Intensive Industries are "Free Riders"

In Chapter 1, we used lights in a tunnel to simulate the mass market. Let's try a slightly different analogy now. Imagine that the mass market consists of a "river" of consumer purchasing power. Along the banks of this river are located industries of all types.

When an industry sells a product or service to consumers in the market, it pumps purchasing power *from* the river. An industry also pumps purchasing power *back into* the river in two primary ways: first it pays salaries and wages to workers, and second as technology advances, the prices that the industry charges fall and this results in more money in consumers' pockets. As we have seen, however, at some point, the industries on the banks of our river will become *too capital intensive* (the machines they employ will begin to run themselves). Once this happens, they will collectively begin to pump more purchasing power from the river than they return to it. The river will begin to run dry.

In the case of a real-world river, we would never advocate allowing a business or industry to pump unlimited quantities of water from the river without bearing the appropriate costs associated with preserving that public resource. A business that somehow circumvented the regulations or costs associated with the use of the river would be considered a "free rider." In economic terms, a free rider is someone who jumps on the bus—or utilizes any public resource—without paying the fare.

Economists do not consider the market itself to be a public resource. However, I will argue that the market (or the collective purchasing power of consumers) is really *the ultimate public resource*. It is the resource from which virtually all wealth in a free market economy derives. Think of the words you might use to describe a business that you admire: "well-managed," "innovative," "efficient." Within the context of our river analogy, all these things amount to building a better pump. Obviously, a great pump positioned next to a dry riverbed doesn't have much value. When a business becomes highly capital intensive and employs few workers, it becomes a free rider relative to the market resource. This is true in terms of purchasing power returned to the market and also in terms of its tax burden.

Imagine a fully automated factory. The only contribution such a factory would make to our purchasing power river would be by creating products at a lower price. No wages would be paid. No payroll taxes would be paid. While lower prices would return some purchasing power to the river, this would simply not be enough. Over time, as all industries become less labor intensive, the river will run dry.

In the future, we will need government policies that recognize this reality. We will need policies that prevent the market river from running dry. In the long run, if advanced machine automation permanently disenfranchises a significant fraction of the work force, we will have no choice except to make some significant changes to our economic system so that the free market can continue to function. That will be the subject of the next chapter. In the meantime, our objective should be to stabilize the system and ensure that the job losses due to automation are as gradual as possible. The most important short-term goal is to avoid the severe downturn and potentially catastrophic spiral that could result if consumers someday lose confidence in their future income continuity.

The Problem with Payroll Taxes

Whenever a business hires a worker, it takes on the additional burden of payroll taxes on the wages or salary paid to that worker. Payroll taxes are the primary method for funding public retirement, unemployment insurance, and in many countries, health care. In the U.S., payroll taxes include one half of the contribution to Social Security and Medicare, as well as state and federal unemployment insurance.

These taxes create a significant disincentive to hire and retain workers. As the capability of machine automation approaches that of workers, payroll taxes will give employers an even greater incentive to eliminate jobs—or avoid hiring new workers—as quickly as possible. This is especially true in Europe, where payroll taxes are significantly higher than in the U.S. and where it is generally more difficult for companies to lay off workers once they are hired.

The payroll tax-based system will come under tremendous strain in the coming years as a demographic shift results in a large number of retirees supported by relatively fewer workers. In the United States, nearly everyone is aware that Social Security, and especially Medicare, are at high risk of becoming insolvent in the coming decades. In Europe and in Japan, the situation is generally even worse. It is very difficult to see how the generous public pension programs in European countries will continue to be sustainable under a payroll tax-based system. The situation will be far more dire if the trends projected in this book come into play. If in addition to these demographic realities, broad-based automation of jobs unfolds simultaneously, the entire payroll tax-based system seems very likely to fall apart.

As we saw in the previous section, capital intensive industries which enjoy access to the market while employing relatively few workers are not bearing their fair share of the costs associated with maintaining a viable consumer market. Such industries are also avoiding the costs associated with payroll tax-funded social welfare programs. In a very real sense, capital intensive industries are stealing from our purchasing power river and circumventing their responsibility to society.

We can see then that the whole idea of funding social programs via payroll taxes is fundamentally flawed and outdated. It puts an unfair burden on labor intensive industries while allowing capital intensive industries to free ride. That, of course, creates a tremendous incentive for every industry to become more capital intensive as quickly as possible.

This problem also makes the funding of social programs highly susceptible to demographic imbalances. The solution is to get away from the idea of *counting workers* and *taxing based on workers*. We need to instead fund social programs with a different form of tax—a tax that falls fairly on both capital and labor intensive industries and which will be sustainable even as automation increasingly encroaches in the future. Taxation should be based on a business's success in utilizing the market resource, rather than on the number of workers it happens to employ.

The "Workerless" Payroll Tax

If we are going to get rid of payroll taxes, then we obviously have to come up with a viable alternative. We need a tax that falls fairly on every business that enjoys access to the market—regardless of the number of workers employed. A simple solution might be to just get rid of payroll taxes and instead increase general business income taxes. This is probably the right direction in which to move, but the problem is that businesses only pay income taxes when they are profitable. Payroll taxes have to be paid regardless of year-to-year profitability. Obviously, the government needs a reliable revenue stream in order to fund social programs.

For this reason, I would suggest that a good alternative might be some form of *gross margin tax*. The gross margin of a business is a measure of its basic operating profitability. Essentially it is equal to revenue less cost of goods sold. Gross margins vary a great deal by industry, so it would probably be necessary to adjust the tax based on the dynamics of individual industry sectors. Nonetheless, it should be possible to come up with a relatively simple formula for a gross margin tax that would raise the same amount of revenue as the current payroll tax system while distributing the tax burden fairly among industries. For the vast majority of businesses the gross margin will always be positive, and a minimum could be enforced if necessary to ensure a reliable revenue stream.

Under this new system, businesses would pay two types of taxes just as they do currently: (1) They would pay a gross margin tax *instead* of the current payroll tax, and (2) they would continue to pay the normal business income tax. Consider some of the advantages of this system:

- Since payroll taxes would be eliminated, the incentive to automate jobs or move them overseas would immediately be reduced. Likewise, the prospect of hiring a new worker would immediately become more attractive.
- A business that did choose to automate or offshore jobs would *not* be able to avoid contributing to the social programs that support the population.

- The demographic, or "baby boom," issue would be mitigated because we would be moving away from a model based on counting workers and toward a model where overall economic activity supports social programs.
- The new revenue system would provide an obvious mechanism for funding universal health care in the U.S. without creating yet another incentive to eliminate workers.

It is important to note that a gross margin tax would, of course, only work in the for-profit sector. In other employment sectors a different scheme would need to be used, or perhaps payroll taxes could be retained.

"Progressive" Wage Deductions

As this book is being written, there is significant public outcry over the issue of excessive paychecks for corporate CEOs. One of the basic messages I have tried to express is that extreme income inequality and concentration of income is not simply an issue of fairness. In fact, it drives at the very heart of a functional mass market. As we have mentioned previously, if you consider nearly any moderately priced mass market product or service, an average worker contributes nearly as much to the viability of that market as a corporate CEO. An extremely wealthy individual may purchase a very nice car, or perhaps even several cars. But he or she is not going to purchase 100 or 1000 automobiles. When income is too concentrated, it undermines the mass market. That is a reality that ultimately will affect everyone—and the corporate CEOs of the future are going to find themselves on the frontline when the wave hits.

Currently, businesses in the United States can deduct all wage and salary expenses when calculating corporate income taxes. No consideration is given to how that deduction is distributed among workers. This simply makes no sense.

I would suggest that a significant job creation incentive could be established if we instead used a *progressive schedule* for deductions. This would work in a somewhat similar fashion to the progressive[47] tax brackets we now have—except that it would apply to deductions. Here is an example that is intended only as a very simple illustration. Employers might be allowed to deduct *twice* the amount paid to workers making up to $50,000. From $50,001 to $200,000 a full deduction would be allowed. From $200,001 to $400,000 half the amount could be deducted. And beyond $400,000 no deduction would be allowed.

So for example:

- For a worker earning $50,000, twice this amount, or $100,000 could be deducted.
- For a worker earning $150,000, $200,000 could be deducted (2 × $50,000 + $100,000)
- For a worker earning $400,000, $350,000 could be deducted (2 × $50,000 + $150,000 + $200,000/2)
- For a CEO earning $20 million, a maximum of only $350,000 could be deducted.

The basic problem with executive pay is that it creates an *excessive and wasteful incentive*. Suppose that CEOs were able to earn a maximum of only $10 million per year (including bonuses). Would there suddenly be an extreme shortage of corporate CEOs? Would no one want to be a CEO? It's possible that a few CEOs who have already acquired substantial wealth might decide to just play golf, but by and large, I think it is evident that being a corporate CEO would remain a pretty attractive option.

The fact is that such enormous paychecks are simply not necessary in order to attract talent to these positions. The huge paychecks come about because of corporate cronyism, where executives sit on the boards of each other's companies, and also because of competition between companies. A board that does not offer an outsized pay package may well fear that the CEO will go to a competitor. This is clearly not a healthy or necessary dynamic for the economy as a whole, and it is really not something that should be encouraged by tax policy. Obviously, if progressive wage deductions were implemented, this would have an impact on the total amount of revenue collected. To address that we might need to adjust the overall tax rate so that the changes are, at a minimum, revenue neutral.

Defeating the Lobbyists

In Chapter 2, I made the point that information technology is advancing at a geometric (or exponential) rate. Unfortunately, there is also something else that is accelerating geometrically: the number of lobbyists in Washington.[48] The federal tax code offers one of the few available opportunities to design specific incentives that might result in significant job creation. The system of progressive wage deductions that I proposed earlier is just one example of such an incentive; others with experience in taxation could no doubt suggest other ideas. However, any such effort to leverage the tax code seems very unlikely to survive the influence of the special interest groups that now dominate the legislative process.

In his book *The Future of Freedom: Illiberal Democracy at Home and Abroad*, Fareed Zakaria makes the point that the ever increasing power that lobbyists and special interests wield is at least in part due to laws which force every aspect of the legislative process into the open. While, on the surface, it may appear that openness in government is always desirable and more democratic, the reality is that very few of us have the time, energy or attention span to take an active interest in the intricate and mundane details of the legislative process. The people who *do* take active advantage of this transparency tend to be the ones who have a very significant vested interest in the legislation being considered. Lobbyists are able to follow every vote in every committee and can immediately exert influence whenever they see the slightest hint of something they don't like. This has led to dramatically reduced opportunities for the type of behind the scenes bargaining and compromise that was once an integral part of the political process. The end result is a more partisan Congress and a lot less consensus.

One very interesting idea that offers at least a partial solution to this problem has been proposed by economist Alan S. Blinder.[49] He has suggested the creation of an independent agency, similar to the Federal Reserve, which would have the authority to specify the details of the tax code. Congress would maintain its overall constitutional authority over taxation, but the details would be removed from the political process and instead handled by a board of highly skilled professionals.

The current financial situation has clearly demonstrated the absolute necessity of having a central bank with the authority to respond rapidly in times of crisis. While not everyone may agree with the wisdom of each specific action taken by the Federal Reserve as the crisis has unfolded, very few would dispute the fact that these initiatives have been extraordinarily creative and have been executed with a timeliness that few other branches of government could hope to match. We would not want to imagine a scenario in which the actions undertaken independently by the Fed instead required a vote in Congress.

In the future, technological change is likely to continue to cause increasingly disruptive changes in the economy. We have already seen how the availability of powerful computers made it possible for Wall Street technicians to create new, exotic forms of tradable securities and how this led directly to the severity of the global financial crisis. Unanticipated economic and financial impacts such as this will almost certainly become more common as technology continues to progress. Given this, we simply cannot afford to have a government that runs on only one cylinder. We need a government with the flexibility to leverage all the tools at its disposal in times of rapid change or crisis. Getting the details of the tax code, and perhaps other critical facets of government operation, away from the direct, detail-level influence of Washington lobbyists would be a very important first step in the right direction.

A More Conventional View of the Future

Many of the ideas presented so far in this book are unconventional; many people may even feel that they are radical. If you visit any bookstore or library, you can easily find a dozen or more books, often written by well-known authors, that present an entirely different, and perhaps more palatable, forecast of the future. Before you dismiss the ideas presented here, perhaps it would be worthwhile to look in a little more depth at some of the most widely held conventional assumptions about the future and see if they are really reasonable:

- The primary force that will shape the coming decades will be globalization. Offshoring of jobs and the continuing migration of manufacturing to low wage countries will be the major threats to the job market in Western countries. Technology will continue to enable globalization, and jobs will move across borders with increasing ease, but automation technology will not result in broad-based, permanent elimination of jobs. Under pressure from globalization, jobs in the developed economies will evolve increasingly toward providing services that are anchored locally—and neither automation technology nor globalization will succeed in penetrating these protected employment markets.

- Technology will improve the way we communicate and collaborate. It will increasingly allow us to work from home, and many of us will have the opportunity to offer our unique skills directly to the global market on a piecemeal or freelance basis, joining ad-hoc teams of other workers from around the world to work on specific projects. Technology will change our jobs and the way we work; it will allow us to work together in new ways, but it will *never* become capable of *autonomously doing* our jobs.

- Even as artificial intelligence becomes far more sophisticated and as robots are increasingly deployed for military applications and perhaps even as consumer products, the routine and relatively repetitive jobs held by millions of workers in offices, warehouses, supermarkets, retail chain stores and small businesses will remain secure.

- To the extent that any average workers are, in fact, displaced by automation, they will be retrained or re-educated—and the economy will *always* create jobs that will take advantage of those newly acquired skills.

- Future technology will result in the creation of entirely new industries, and these industries will offer new employment opportunities. History has shown that the more technologically advanced an industry is, the more capital intensive it typically is; as a result, it employs relatively few people. This will somehow change in the future, so that millions of new jobs will be available for average workers.

- As technology advances, manufactured products will become far more sophisticated and increasingly miniaturized. Specifications and tolerances will be tighter.

Automation will have to be introduced to make this possible. Nonetheless, factories throughout the world will continue to be relatively labor intensive, and untold millions of third-world workers will continue to migrate from the agrarian economy to the manufacturing sector.

- These third-world factory workers will continue to churn out products that will be largely consumed by people in developed countries. Workers (consumers) in the West—supported by their lucrative online collaboration and piecemeal work—will be eager purchasers of these imports for decades to come.

- Ultimately, it is possible that advanced nanotechnology may begin to be deployed in the manufacturing sector. Nano-manufacturing will involve manipulating matter at the molecular and perhaps even atomic level. Self-replicating "nano-bots" may be designed to build products from the ground up. Nonetheless, all those millions of low wage workers will remain indispensable to the production process.

Does this view of the future really seem more likely—more down to earth—than what I have presented? Can we expect this forecast to hold true decade after decade as technology continues advancing at its geometric pace? The reality seems to be that most people who forecast the future either cannot imagine, or are not willing to consider, a world in which human workers become increasingly superfluous. Economy-wide automation of jobs is not a technological impossibility; it is a *psychological* impossibility.[']

Many people will dismiss the ideas presented here primarily on a historical basis. Because this has never happened before, it can never happen in the future. The problem with this is that, as we saw in Chapter 2, the geometric acceleration of information technology is sure to have a disruptive impact on the historical trend line. As it says in every mutual fund advertisement and prospectus, "Past performance is not a predictor of future results."

It is especially easy to be dismissive because similar arguments have been put forth many times in the past. The Luddites, of course, raised the alarm a bit prematurely in 1811. Over the years, organized labor has on various occasions pointed out the threat from automation. In his 1995 book, *The End of Work*,[50] Jeremy Rifkin gives many examples of the social impact that job automation has already had and speculates that, in the future, it may lead to social disintegration, dramatic rises in crime, civil unrest and possibly even the fall of governments. The alarm has been raised, but so far the wolf has not shown up. Does that really mean that the wolf is only an illusion?

['] It's always very dangerous to use the word "impossible" where technology is concerned. History has shown this again and again. One famous example is Lord Kelvin, the inventor of the Kelvin temperature scale and one of the preeminent scientists of his day. Kelvin declared that flight by heavier than air machines was impossible or at best completely impractical. This was just a few years before the Wright brothers built the first airplane.

The Risk of Inaction

At the beginning of this chapter, I suggested that a disastrous economic downturn could result if a critical mass of consumers begins to anticipate broad-based, permanent job loss due to automation technologies and globalization at some point in the future. If such a trend does develop, it seems clear that only the government has the ability to implement policies to address the situation. The natural incentives in the private sector would tend to accelerate, rather than resolve, the crisis.

There is an ongoing trend toward concentration of income that is driven largely by the continuing advance of automation technology and globalization, and also by a lack of progressive tax policies. Many people might argue that increasing income inequality is caused primarily by a "skill premium." In other words, in the modern, technological economy, people who are highly educated and skilled have a significant advantage in the labor force. While this has been true so far, it is largely because relatively low skill jobs have been the *first to be automated* and also the first to be subjected to the full force of globalization. As we saw in Chapter 2, advancing automation technology will increasingly threaten highly paid knowledge workers with college educations. These jobs will also, of course, be subject to offshoring. Clear evidence of these trends is already apparent in information technology (IT) jobs, and we can expect this to become much more broad-based in the future. We can expect that income will become even more concentrated in the hands of those who are positioned to benefit directly from the increasing value of technological capital relative to labor.

Extreme income inequality is generally presented as a social problem or an issue of basic fairness. While it may be these things, it is also—more critically—a *mathematical* problem in terms of the viability of the mass market. When purchasing power is taken from thousands of average consumers and concentrated in the hands of one wealthy individual, that purchasing power is effectively sterilized: it no longer plays a vibrant role in generating mass market demand for products and services. As we have seen, this will ultimately cause the market "river" to run dry.

We often hear that income in the United States is today more concentrated than at any time since the 1920s. The reality is that the risks from this concentration are probably even higher today because the rise of the mass market has changed the nature of our economy. Today, virtually everyone in industrialized society—including especially the most wealthy individuals—derives his or her income directly or indirectly from the mass market.

The social impact resulting from the permanent elimination of a large fraction of the jobs held by average people would obviously be dramatic. History shows that once unemployment reaches a certain level, the very foundations of democratic society may be threatened. During the Great Depression, unemployment reached 25 percent in the United States. Joseph P. Kennedy, the founder of the Kennedy dynasty, famously said that during this period, he would have gladly given up half of everything he had, if he could have been certain of retaining the other half of his fortune under the rule of law. Clearly, the risks are very real, not just for the bulk of people whose incomes may be threatened, but also for those wealthy individuals who may be likely to resist the idea of government policies that include more progressive taxation.

My purpose in writing this book is to try to give these issues more visibility in the hope that a constructive discussion and debate can occur. Perhaps the arguments that I have presented here will turn out to be wrong. But if they are even partially correct, then we cannot afford to be taken by surprise; it will be essential to have a plan.

In the next chapter, we will fast forward to a point in the future where the trend toward widespread job automation has become clear. Once this happens, there will really be no choice except to come up with some modifications to our system so that the free market can continue to function and thrive.

Chapter 4

TRANSITION

In the previous chapters of this book, we have seen that machine automation is likely to someday eliminate a substantial fraction of the jobs now performed by people. Automation is poised to advance on two broad fronts. First, machines and robots will increasingly take over the routine jobs in factories, retail stores, offices and warehouses that are now held by workers.

Second, the existing trend toward technology-enabled self-service will accelerate. We already see this trend with ATMs, automated checkout aisles, online banking, and automated telephone answering systems. All of these represent areas where machines allow consumers to independently perform tasks that once required the involvement of human workers. In the future, we can expect that this trend will be extended to include cell phones and other mobile devices so that consumers will be able perform tasks and get automated assistance almost anywhere.

In addition, the drive toward self-service will also occur *within* businesses. New automation tools will enable managers in both large corporations and small businesses to directly do the jobs and perform the analysis that once required human employees.

As we saw in the last chapter, if these trends become unambiguous and are allowed to impact in an uncontrolled manner, the result is likely to be a severe economic downturn as workers (who are also consumers) begin to fear for their long-term employment prospects. In Chapter 3, I proposed some initiatives which might help to stabilize the situation and delay the onset of this scenario; however, we cannot escape the fact that technological advance is relentless and that free market incentives will continue to push the private sector toward the elimination of jobs. Once we accept the fact that a large fraction of jobs will be automated in the future, then we really have no choice but to also accept the reality that our economic system, as it exists today, cannot continue to function indefinitely without modification.

In this chapter, we are going to fast forward far into the future; we will imagine a time when at least three quarters of the jobs which exist in our current economy have been permanently automated away. In other words, the unemployment rate will be at least 75 percent—an almost unimaginably high level—and there will be *no* realistic hope that more jobs will be created in the future. Is it possible to have a prosperous economy and a civil society in such a scenario?

If we can devise a system that would work in such an admittedly extreme situation, then we should also be able to figure out a way to gradually transition into that new system, so that we can maintain economic stability as automation advances in the coming years and decades. Toward that end, let's begin by looking at the basic elements of our existing free market economy.

The Basis of the Free Market Economy: Incentives

The free market economy is a natural system that pushes consumers, businesses, investors and workers to act in ways that ultimately propel society as a whole toward advancement and greater prosperity. In other words, as each of us pursues our own self-interest, collectively we move everyone forward. Through the logic of the market, these collective actions automatically allocate resources in the most efficient way so that economic output is maximized. This, of course, is the "invisible hand" that Adam Smith spoke of.

We can divide the logic of the free market into three broad sets of incentives:

1. Individual consumers act to find the best values for products and services. In other words, consumers shop around. No one wants to overpay, and no one wants to end up with an inferior product.
2. The owners of businesses and capital compete to maximize profits by providing the best possible value to consumers. As they do so, they invest in ways that drive innovation and create new products, services and industries.
3. Individual workers act to maximize their income. They seek the best possible job, invest in education and

training to enhance their future career prospects, and do their current job to the best of their ability.

Historically, these three incentives have worked in concert to drive society toward ever increasing prosperity. As we have seen, the problem we face if automation eliminates a large fraction of the jobs held by workers is that consumers and workers are *the same individuals*. Without reliable income from employment, there will no longer be a critical mass of viable consumers. And it is consumers who ultimately drive the mass market economy. Without the expectation of sufficient market demand, no rational business owner will invest in increased production or innovation.

Preserving the Market

Clearly, in order to preserve the mass market in a largely automated economy, we need to provide an alternative to jobs. We need a mechanism that can get a reliable income stream into the hands of consumers. This of course, is a proposition that will be very difficult for most of us to accept; the idea that we must work for a living is one of our most basic core values. The current alternatives to job-based income, such as unemployment insurance or welfare payments, come with highly negative connotations and are purposely designed to provide minimal support so that a disincentive to work is not established.

Our current value system celebrates the importance of our labor. We believe that work is essential and that consumption is a privilege that derives from that work. However, this is a belief system that is fundamentally based on the historical reality that human labor is indispensable to the production process. What happens when technology reaches the point where most human labor is no longer essential?

At that point, we will have to undergo a quantum shift in our value system. In order to preserve the free market system, we will have to come to the realization that while work (at least for most people) may no longer be essential, *broad-based consumption is essential.* In the developed world, our mass market economy has grown far beyond what is required to simply provide individuals with basic necessities. In order to maintain the global economy and drive it toward future growth, we must have a very large number of consumers with adequate purchasing power—all of whom have confidence in their future continuity of income. Without that critical mass of viable consumers, economic decline is mathematically inescapable.

There is really no way to envision how the private sector can solve this problem. There is simply no real alternative except for the government to provide some type of income mechanism for consumers. While this idea will initially, of course, be vehemently opposed, I believe that in time, this will have to be accepted as a basic function of government.

Consider the viewpoint of an economically conservative or libertarian thinker. This person is likely to advocate the smallest possible government and a market that is as free and unregulated as possible. Nonetheless, this person—if he or she is reasonable—is very unlikely to propose eliminating government entirely because he or she understands that there is one core function of government which is critical to the operation of the free market: the protection of property rights. The government must maintain a national defense, a police force and a judicial system, and it must enforce and protect clearly defined rights to own and trade property. Without these governmental functions, the free market could not operate effectively and civil society would erode into jungle warfare.

In a future, largely automated economy, the preservation of robust market demand by providing an income stream to individual consumers will also have to become a core function of government. This is an idea that will no doubt initially elicit derision or outrage. In the long run, however, I believe that there will simply be no alternative.

Market demand powers our economy. No rational business owner will invest in increased production in the absence of an expectation of demand. In the economic environment of 2009, consumerism is very much out of fashion, and this is really not a good thing. The media is replete with stories about how Americans have gone out and spent too much on big screen TVs. These stories miss the point. While there will always be some individuals who act irresponsibly, the overall problem is really not that Americans have spent too much. The problem is that their spending has been sustained by borrowing rather than by growth in real income. And this is because, for most average people, there has been little or no growth in income, while at the same time, health care costs have been exploding.

In the long run, *only* sustained consumer spending can turn the economy around and return us to economic growth. Everything produced by our economy is ultimately consumed by individual people; we cannot have long-term prosperity unless enormous numbers of people have sufficient income—and sufficient confidence in the future—to power sustained consumption.

Again, conservative economic thinkers may reflexively object to this view. Conservatives tend to emphasize the importance of production (or the "supply side") in the natural cycle that occurs between production and consumption. Conservatives generally favor low taxes and minimum regulation of producers in the expectation that this will result in increased economic activity and job creation, which will then lead to strong consumer demand. The problem with that way of thinking, of course, is that, in an increasingly automated economy, the job creation will not occur. Consumers will have little opportunity to participate in the production process as workers and will lose access to the wages that sustain them. In the absence of an alternate income mechanism, a collapse in consumer spending must be the inevitable result.

Recapturing Wages

As we begin to envision how it might be possible to design an alternative income stream for consumers, let's begin by considering how the wages from a job that has been automated away could be recaptured by the government. When a business eliminates a job as the result of automation technology, the income that was previously paid to that worker does not simply vaporize. In fact, it is redirected in two ways: (1) Some of the income accrues to the owners and managers of the business, and (2) some of the income is redirected to the consumers of the business's products or services in the form of lower prices.

Therefore, the government can recapture the wages from the automated job with some combination of two types of taxes. First, higher business taxes, capital gains taxes and more progressive income taxes on wealthy individuals can be used to recapture the income that goes to the business's owners. The gross margin tax proposed in the previous chapter or a carbon tax might also provide effective mechanisms for recapturing some of this income. Secondly, some form of consumption tax could be used to recapture that portion of the lost wages that results in lower prices. This consumption tax might be a simple sales tax[1] or a value added tax (VAT) similar to the ones already popular in Europe.

Once again, these ideas will probably be met with strong resistance. Wealthy individuals and business owners will initially be very unhappy. However, a business manager in the future will ultimately have to face two alternatives: (1) A new form of taxation designed to redirect income to consumers, or (2) catastrophically falling demand. This is really not a difficult choice. In an automated economy, low tax rates and robust demand are going to be fundamentally incompatible. In the absence of the jobs

---

[1] If a sales tax is used it should certainly be an internal tax that is incorporated into the total price (similar to gasoline taxes) rather than an external tax that is tacked onto the total (like state sales taxes).

that currently power consumers, some new form of taxation will be essential for creating an income mechanism that leads to sustained demand for products and services.

It is very important to note that I am not advocating taxes so high that *all value* from technological progress is recaptured. As technology advances, it provides benefits far beyond simply eliminating jobs. Innovation results in new products and services and creates entirely new and very lucrative markets. Consider the case of a fully automated factory. As technology progresses, the factory will continue to become even more efficient and produce products at lower prices, even though all the jobs have already been eliminated. The taxes I have proposed are intended *only* to recapture the wages from jobs that have been automated away. In other words, the higher taxes will simply replace the wages that would have been paid in the absence of automation. Beyond this, the owners of the business will continue to benefit from their investments in improved technology. To see this, consider the table that follows.

Unit Cost Breakdown for a Hypothetical Product or Service

	Current Cost	Future Cost (no wage recapture)	Future Cost (with wage recapture)
Cost of non-executive wages	$40	$10	$10
Conventional Taxes	$15	$15	$15
Special new taxes to recapture wage income	$0	$0	$30
Other Costs	$45	$35	$35
Total Unit Cost	$100	$60	$90

The table above offers a hypothetical and admittedly simplistic example of a product or service that has a current unit cost of $100.[1] The table shows that $40 of this currently represents wages paid to non-executive employees. Over time, as automation progresses, the portion of the unit cost allocated to wages falls to $10. Notice, however, that the "other costs" category also falls. This represents the cost benefits of advancing technology, which are distinct from the elimination of wages. The goal should be to impose a tax that recaptures the lost wages, without also capturing the additional non-wage related benefits of innovation. In this example, we have recaptured all of the lost wages. In reality, we might want to impose a some-

---

[1] For simplicity, I have expressed this idea in terms of per-unit cost. In practice, it would be better to base the wage recapture scheme on wages as a percentage of *total* revenue for the business.

what lower tax on businesses and then use an additional consumption tax to capture the remaining wage income. This strategy will ensure that the business continues to see a meaningful incentive to innovate.

One approach to this problem might be to develop historical wage guidelines for each type of business based on industry, business size, etc. As automation increases, the wage recapture taxes would be gradually raised so that the total of wages paid and wage recapture taxes remained relatively constant as a percentage of revenue over time. The government would keep the revenues raised from these special taxes completely separate from the revenues it uses for its normal operations. The revenue from these taxes would then be used exclusively to replace income from lost wages.

It would also be possible to design a wage recapture scheme which de-emphasizes direct taxes on business and relies more on a consumption tax. The problems with this are that the tax would need to be very high and would be regressive (it would fall most heavily on those with low incomes). However, this could be addressed partly by charging a lower tax rate on necessities and a higher tax rate on luxury goods. It should also be combined with more progressive income taxation on individuals. A strategy relying more on a consumption tax would have the advantage of not making domestic producers less competitive with their international counterparts. Any significant consumption tax would have to be imposed equally on Internet sales and would require the creation of a mechanism for insuring that taxes were paid on items being shipped from overseas (otherwise sales would simply gravitate to offshore merchants). The consumption tax would also either have to apply to services as well as tangible products, or service providers would need to be subject to a direct wage recapture tax.[1]

The ideas I am presenting here, of course, represent only a basic framework. The details and the tradeoffs between various types and levels of taxation would need to be worked out using extensive analysis and probably through computer simulation of the economy. Obviously, any real world taxes that we implement in order to recapture the income from automated jobs will end up doing so in an imperfect way. We also know that government tends to be inefficient and wasteful. However, that does not change the reality of the situation. Since government is the only entity that can impose overall regulation and collect taxes, there is no realistic alternative to some form of government involvement.

One essential principle of any such scheme to recapture wage income is that the revenues raised must be kept separate. An absolute firewall should be established between this special function of government and the funds used for general government operation. This should be made easier by the fact that the funds would be immediately distributed to consumers; there would not be any long-term fund that could be raided and used for other

---

[1] It might also be necessary to have different tax rates for different products or services based on labor content. For a service that remained labor intensive, the rate could be lower since wages were already being paid. For a highly automated service the tax rate would be higher.

purposes. A second important point we can make is that, eventually, this special and separate government function would subsume many of the activities now provided for by other government programs. Welfare, unemployment insurance and even social security could ultimately be replaced by this new, separately managed, income scheme. That would leave a far smaller government core.

Positive Aspects of Jobs

While it is conceptually not difficult to envision how the government might recapture lost wages through special taxes, it is much harder to design an effective way to direct that income to consumers in the absence of jobs. In fact, the incentives attached to jobs provide many benefits beyond income, both to individuals and to society as a whole:

- Jobs provide a useful occupation for our time. They provide individuals with a sense of purpose, and they result in a more orderly and civil society.
- Jobs provide hope for advancement. Even those workers in the lowest paid professions can hope that they will someday be afforded a better opportunity. The presence of this hope for the future is an important component of stability—both for an individual's emotional state and for society in general. Belief in the possibility of a better future is also a significant driver of current consumption.
- Jobs motivate people to invest in education, training and other forms of self improvement. An individual's primary incentive for such an investment

may be the promise of a better career, but both the individual and society as a whole derive many ancillary benefits.

Clearly, if we are to come up with an alternative income mechanism, it is essential that these incentives somehow be preserved. The lack of these incentives is a primary problem with current welfare programs. Welfare, as it is currently implemented, provides few incentives for self improvement and little hope for the future. It tends to result in a permanent underclass, and it certainly does not create the type of viable consumers that we need to power the economy of the future.

The Power of Inequality

The idea of incentives is closely tied to the concept of income inequality. In this book, I have made the point that extreme income concentration and inequality will ultimately undermine the viability of the mass market. However, it is important to note that the other extreme also presents very serious problems. A program in which everyone is provided with a relatively equal income—in return for doing nothing—provides no motivation for self improvement, no sense of self-worth and no hope for a better future. This is the problem with existing welfare programs.

What we need then is a mechanism that provides for *unequal* (but not unfair) incomes. We need to synthetically recreate the rewards and incentives that are currently tied to jobs. The ideal is to provide unequal income but equal opportunity, so that every individual can have a realistic expectation of advancing his or her position. Most importantly, we need to ensure that the incentives built into the system motivate individuals to do what is best for themselves and for society as a whole.

Where the Free Market Fails: Externalities

While there is little question that the free market offers the best overall efficiency of any known economic system, it is nonetheless an imperfect system. Perhaps the biggest shortcoming of the free market economy is in the area of *externalities.* An externality is a cost (or benefit) which falls on society as a whole, but which is not incorporated into the individual incentives faced by businesses and individuals.

A classic example of an externality is industrial pollution. In the absence of government regulation, it costs a factory nothing to simply dump toxic waste into the environment. In fact, the natural operation of the free market would drive even environmentally conscious business managers to pollute because, if they decided to unilaterally bear the extra costs of handling waste properly, they would find themselves at a competitive disadvantage. For this reason, governments enforce regulations regarding toxic waste and pollution.

The most significant externality that society will have to deal with in the coming decades is, of course, climate change brought on by uncontrolled carbon emissions. In the near future, we can hope that regulations or taxes will increasingly be implemented to help address this issue.

In general, governments have reasonable success enforcing laws that help minimize negative externalities at the industry level, but it is much harder to effectively address externalities at the individual consumer level. This is a huge problem because the day-to-day choices made by billions of people throughout the world obviously have an enormous collective impact on the environment.

Because you care about the environment, you may be drawn to the idea of replacing your older, fuel inefficient car with a newer hybrid model. While this may save you some money on gasoline, you will quickly realize that once you factor in other costs, such as depreciation, the transaction probably does not make sense on a purely financial basis. In fact, individual incentives for acting in environmentally conscious ways are typically quite weak. While public education does succeed in motivating many people to make the right choices in terms of the cars they drive, or a decision to use public transit, or participation in recycling programs, there is little doubt that far better results could be obtained if the incentives were somehow stronger.

Your income depends on your job, and so you are sure to wake up in the morning and arrive at work on time. That is a powerful incentive. What if your income also depended to some extent on your behaviors relative to the environment? Clearly, that would cause a dramatic readjustment in the priority that we all give to acting in environmentally responsible ways.

While designing a system that replaces the idea of a traditional job with some other mechanism for delivering income to consumers is a serious challenge, we can now see that it also presents an enormous opportunity. Clearly, we will want to incorporate incentives that directly address environmental issues (and other externalities) into our new income mechanism.[']

Creating a Virtual Job

At the most basic level, a job is essentially a set of incentives. As a person acts according to those incentives, he or she performs work that is currently required in order to produce products and services. In the economy of the future, if that work is no longer required, we will need to create "virtual" jobs. In other words, people will continue to earn income by acting in accordance with incentives, but their actions will not necessarily result in "work" in the traditional sense.

The income earned by individuals must be *un*equal and dependent on each individual's success in acting according to the established incentives. This will ensure that people are motivated to act in ways that benefit themselves as well as society as a whole. Most importantly, this system will get a reliable stream of income into the hands of consumers, and as we have seen, that is absolutely essential in order to create sustained demand for mass market products and services and therefore drive the economy. If we can do that successfully, then the free market economy can continue to operate and generate broad-based prosperity indefinitely.

['] Some people might object to the idea of incorporating environmental incentives into income as government intrusion. Remember, however, we are only talking about income that is *provided* by the government. Individuals with private sources of income would be free to ignore the incentives.

The obvious questions that arise next are: What should these incentives be, and who should set them? The basic incentives should be fairly obvious; we simply need to combine the best positive incentives that are currently built into the idea of a traditional job with additional incentives that directly address the externalities that our current system overlooks. I would suggest that the incentives should be roughly as follows:

Education

The most important determinant of income should be the level of education achieved. Individuals with more education should earn more. A more educated population has many benefits to society, including a lower crime rate, greater civic participation, a more informed electorate and a more flourishing cultural environment. In addition, more educated individuals are far more likely to find fulfillment in a future where traditional work takes up a smaller fraction of each person's time.

While automation may eventually eliminate full-time work opportunities for the bulk of the population, there will continue to be a minority of individuals who have the necessary entrepreneurial skills and knowledge to participate actively in driving technological advancement and economic growth. These individuals will require a high degree of education and training. By emphasizing the idea of education for *everyone*, we will maximize the number of such individuals that will become available and, therefore, improve the prospects for continued advancement and prosperity.

I would go further and argue that, in addition to providing incentives for pursuing formal educational degrees, we should create a program that motivates people to routinely acquire knowledge by engaging in continuing education programs or even simply by reading. Recent surveys have shown that the number of people who regularly read books is in continuing decline. Studies have also shown that our population is, in many cases, disturbingly ignorant of even the most basic knowledge. A recent National Science Foundation survey showed that 20 percent of the U.S. population actually believes that the sun is in orbit around the earth![51] Likewise, too many Americans would probably be hard pressed to find Iraq or Afghanistan—two countries in which we are actively engaged in wars—on a map of the world.

At the same time, we seem to be moving increasingly toward a direct democracy model in which a largely uninformed electorate is given influence over detailed government policy. In California, this occurs literally in the form of ballot initiatives, but even at the national level, it happens when politicians adjust their positions based on opinion polls.

There is also strong evidence to suggest that while the Internet provides unprecedented access to information, too many of us, especially among the younger generation, are failing to assimilate that information. The migration toward a society in which a large part of the average person's knowledge of the world resides not in his or her brain, but in online information sources like Wikipedia, is dangerous and unacceptable.[']

Community and Civic Activities

A second set of incentives should be designed to motivate individuals to participate in activities that enhance community, civic and cultural development. In his book, *The End of Work*, Jeremy Rifkin advocates the creation of a "third sector" which would be focused on providing community and social services, and this idea should certainly be incorporated into our incentive scheme. It is likely that in the future, we may see a mix of direct incentive-based income streams and traditional full or part-time jobs.

As automation advances, the remaining traditional jobs are likely to be those that require uniquely human attributes. In the future, we will continue to need social workers, community activists, health care workers, and people who specialize in working with children. By emphasizing education, we will likely create many traditional jobs for teachers at all levels.

['] Incentive incomes could be easily tied to the number of books a person reads. Future technology should make it possible for an artificial intelligence algorithm to scan a book and instantly create a comprehension test. It is, of course, easy to laugh or sneer at the idea that people should be paid to read instead of to work. But, as I have tried to point out here again and again, if we transition into an automated economy, we will have to pay people to do *something*—or we will have a general collapse of consumer demand. Providing our citizens with an incentive to read and become informed is really not a silly utopian idea: it is ultimately a matter of basic national security.

It is important to note that our new economic model will *not* in any way prevent individuals who wish to work and can find positions from doing so and earning additional income. We are simply recognizing that there will not be enough of these jobs for everyone, and that they will not, by themselves, provide an adequate income level for the population. Income earned from traditional jobs should, in general, be in addition to and independent of, the incentive-based income paid by the government. This would ensure that a sufficient incentive exists to attract workers into areas where traditional work is still required.

Journalism

Another area which is related to the idea of civic and community involvement is professional journalism. The framers of the U.S. constitution recognized that the scrutiny of government provided by a free press was essential to freedom, and they acted to ensure that the press was protected from government tyranny.

The framers could not have anticipated, however, that it would ultimately be the Internet, rather than government, that would be the primary threat to the existence of independent journalism. While it is likely that the press will continue to provide effective scrutiny of government at the federal level, we already face a significant risk at the city and local levels. Major cities throughout the United States, which used to support competing newspapers, are now served by only a single publication. In San Francisco, the survival of the only major newspaper is currently at severe risk. The existence of one or more credible and professional publications that shine a continuous light on the actions of government at all levels is critical to effective democracy, and our incentive scheme could recognize this by providing direct support to those who engage in this activity.

The Environment and other Externalities

Finally, our incentive scheme must incorporate the idea of externalities, and the most important of these will be environmental in nature. Individuals who make choices that are positive for the environment should be paid more. By tying income directly to environmentally conscious actions we would create powerful incentives that would minimize our collective negative impact on the planet. By adopting this idea, we have the potential to create a system in which economic prosperity is directly coupled with favorable environmental outcomes. In addition, the system would be flexible enough so that it could be refined to address significant externalities that might arise in the future.[']

[']Another obvious possibility for income incentives is personal health. There are a number of health issues, especially obesity, which have enormous costs for both individuals and society. This, however, is a very tricky area. A simple approach might be to just pay higher incomes to people within a healthy weight range, but this would raise legitimate fairness and discrimination concerns. Another possibility would be to create incentives for healthy behaviors, but this would be difficult to track and verify. In general, health-based incentives would require the government to have access to and track a lot of very personal information, and this would likely raise privacy concerns and the specter of Big Brother. For these reasons, I have relegated health-based incentives to a footnote, but this may be a fertile area for further thought and discussion.

Setting the Incentives

Who should be responsible for defining these incentives and setting the associated income levels? Clearly, this would have to be a function of government, although it might be privatized to some degree (see below). In Chapter 3, I argued that we should consider creating an independent agency to administer the details of the tax code. We would certainly not want our future incentive scheme to be directly influenced by special interests, so it therefore seems likely that the creation of another independent agency would make sense. A "National Incentives Board" could be set up to define and maintain income incentives. This agency would be staffed by professionals and would be able to adjust incentives over time in much the same way that the Federal Reserve controls interest rates.

For those who dislike the idea of a new Fed-like agency, another interesting idea might be to instead give the power to set incomes and incentives to a quasi-private corporation. This would be a corporate entity whose income would be entirely dependent on the overall performance of the economy as measured by a number of broad quantitative parameters. These parameters might include things like economic growth, keeping the distribution of income within reasonable bounds, environmental impact, and the average education level of the population.

It might also be feasible to give every citizen stock in this corporation, perhaps with a long vesting period so that shares could not be rashly sold. Obviously, such a corporation would need to be very highly regulated both in terms of its actions, and in terms of who could own stock and what percentage of ownership would be allowed for any one individual or group. (It would be critical to ensure that the corporation always acted according to the incentives set by the government, rather than in the interests of individuals or groups who controlled a lot of stock.)

While such an entity might offer a somewhat more market-oriented approach to solving the incentive and income problem, the government would still need to regulate the corporation and define the quantitative parameters used to evaluate its performance. Again, we would not want this to be politicized or influenced directly by special interests, so some type of independent government board would probably be required, or perhaps this authority could be given to the Federal Reserve.

Smoothing the Business Cycle and Reducing Economic Risk

Incentive-based income streams provided by the government would largely decouple consumers' income from jobs in the private sector. This would tend to mitigate recessions because job losses would no longer result in substantial cutbacks in consumer spending.

In essence, the effect of moving away from traditional jobs and toward an incentive-based income scheme would be to make the entire economy more robust and less susceptible to unanticipated shocks. As we saw in Chapter 2, accelerating technology has played an important role in making the financial markets more volatile and more vulnerable to unexpected events such as the 2007 subprime meltdown. Once the current global crisis eases, we can be sure that governments will turn to the task of attempting to contain this risk in the future by imposing regulation on the markets. However, the impact of advancing technology will not be confined to just the financial markets. We will ultimately have to address the issue of systemic risk throughout the entire world economy, and this will eventually involve transitioning to a more robust model.

The Market Economy of the Future

The scheme that I have proposed above essentially involves adopting special taxes to recapture the income from lost jobs and then having the government redirect that income according to individual incentives—without the requirement for traditional "work." The conservative reader is likely to violently recoil from this idea. Is this not the worst form of Robin Hood socialism? Am I not proposing to steal from those who have worked hard to build a business and then simply give the proceeds to masses of indolent people in return for doing *nothing*?

I will argue that I am proposing none of these things. Put yourself in the place of a small business owner. Remember that we are still thinking in terms of our extreme future scenario with 75 percent unemployment. How would your business survive in such a situation?

The special wage recapture taxes that you would be required to pay as a business owner would be an inconvenience to you; you would, of course, prefer that you not have to pay them. (The same could be said of the wages you currently pay to your employees.) However, the wage recapture taxes paid by *every other business* will collectively power the consumers that drive your sales (exactly as the wages paid by other businesses do today).

We must find a way to redirect income to large numbers of consumers, or market demand will not be sustainable. It is not necessary to require work for that income because in an automated economy such work will not be required. The recipients of this income will not do "nothing;" they will, in fact, be motivated to behave in ways that benefit us all. The new taxes that I propose are simply a replacement for the wages that would have been paid in a less automated economy.

Without government intervention of this type, free market forces, together with increasing automation, will drive our society toward an unsustainable concentration of income. Imagine a modern, industrialized society in which 95 percent of the population is impoverished and leads a subsistence level existence with little or no discretionary income, while the remaining 5 percent receives nearly all the income. In such a scenario, the majority of industries now in existence would collapse. The businesses from which most wealthy people derive their incomes would fail.

While this is obviously an extreme example, the reality is that economic decline would occur long before such an extreme concentration of income was achieved, and that decline would be accompanied by the deflation of nearly all asset values. The wealthy will not be able to maintain their high incomes by selling things exclusively to each other. The days of the feudal economy are gone. We now have a mass market economy.

As long as an enormous mass market of viable consumers is preserved, the primary incentives that drive the free market economy will remain intact. In the future, it will still be possible to become extremely wealthy by building a new business or product. In fact, it may in some ways, be easier to do so than today. Many business strategists believe that future marketing will increasingly entail selling customized or unique products to huge numbers of small market niches.[52] Evolving online technologies will make it easier to reach the consumers in these tiny niches and offer them highly personalized products and services. This will likely create many opportunities for entrepreneurs and small businesses to create new products geared toward specific market segments. It will also enable large businesses and new industries to sell huge numbers of different products on a highly targeted basis.

However, it should be obvious that the existence of a huge number of viable market niches depends on a robust and ever expanding universe of consumers. In order to provide future entrepreneurs with a rich market for new ventures, we have to somehow ensure that the average consumers in our population have access to reliable income streams even as traditional jobs are increasingly automated away.

Consider the business model of an Internet company like Google. Google relies on revenue from online advertisements that are highly targeted. The advertisers who use Google's system do so because they have confidence that their ads will attract viable consumers with adequate discretionary income. In today's economy, nearly all of those consumers rely on jobs. If at some point in the future, it became obvious that the universe of viable consumers was substantially diminished, advertisers would be far less interested and Google's business model would clearly be threatened.

History has shown that only a select minority of the population has the combination of skill, entrepreneurship, access to capital, and luck that is required to start and run a successful business. This reality will not change: most people are destined to be buyers rather than sellers. The individuals who do succeed in building businesses in the future will likely find that wages paid to employees account for a far smaller fraction of their expenses. However, they will have to pay higher taxes to compensate for this; otherwise, they will not enjoy vibrant market demand for the products and services they create.

An International View

Many people might object to the ideas presented here on the grounds that if a country, such as the United States, were to raise business taxes substantially it would become less competitive relative to other countries and would therefore attract less investment. If you look back at the table on page 165, which showed how a wage recapture tax might affect the unit cost of a hypothetical product or service, the unit cost is clearly higher after taxes to recapture lost wages are implemented. For products or services that face international competition, this would constitute a problem. One solution might be to rely more on a consumption tax rather that a direct business tax. In countries such as the United States, of course, the manufacturing sector has already largely migrated overseas and employment has become increasingly service oriented. In the U.S., the greatest danger is going occur when the service sector automates, and direct foreign competition is less of an issue in that arena.

In the long run, job automation will clearly be a worldwide phenomenon. No country will escape its impact, and this includes developing nations with low wages. As I pointed out in the previous chapter, we are likely to see a shift in the incentives that drive businesses to choose where they invest. Political stability, minimized transportation and energy costs, and proximity to sustained consumption markets will be primary issues in the future.

In the broader sense, we can speculate that an automated economy would, in many ways, redefine the nature of global trade. Some trade between countries occurs because of the availability of natural or agricultural resources (oil or French wine, for example), but much trade occurs because of labor dynamics. If a particular country has low wages and/or a particularly skilled workforce, it currently enjoys an advantage that will lead to trade. In an automated economy, where workers play a far less significant role, this trade dynamic would obviously be less important.

There are really only two primary reasons that the government of a country would want to attract factories and business investment: jobs and taxation. As automation reduces the number of jobs, taxation will become increasingly important. It seems likely that once this issue becomes apparent, some degree of cooperation between nations will develop. Perhaps international entities such as the World Trade Organization will address this issue by setting standards for taxation. We cannot expect that the transition to a new model would be entirely smooth, and perhaps in some cases, protectionist measures will be necessary. While free trade may be desirable, it should clearly be a lower priority than the preservation of our entire economic model.

Transitioning to the New Model

Now that we have seen how the government might be able to support the consumers of the future by redirecting incentive-based income streams captured through taxation, we can begin to think about how to transition into this new model. The primary problem we face is that the current economy is still highly reliant on human labor. We need to develop a system that avoids creating a disincentive to perform necessary work. In other words, we don't want to create inequities by requiring some people to work and not others, and we don't want a "moral hazard" that pushes people to avoid work and seek government support instead.

The answer must be some type of job sharing solution. The exact mechanics of this solution would need to vary depending on the nature of the job. For many job types, it might be possible to simply move toward a part time work schedule so that more people are employed doing the same amount of work. For jobs that do not lend themselves to part time work, a rotation scheme could be used. A worker might rotate into a job on a monthly or even a yearly basis. Jobs could be shared by giving workers a sabbatical at different times of the year.

In each case, workers would be supported by supplementary incentive-based income streams from the government. As automation progresses and more jobs are eliminated, this supplementary income stream will become an increasingly important component of total income. In large corporations and organizations, it might be possible to handle job rotations internally. In smaller businesses, it would probably be necessary to set up external mechanisms so that workers could rotate between employers. Obviously, regulations and/or incentives[1] would be required to implement these job sharing schemes.

Needless to say, the business community is likely to initially oppose this idea and dismiss it as expensive and unworkable. As I've pointed out however, businesses will ultimately have to choose between government intervention and taxation and the existence of a robust market. Once this tradeoff becomes clear, opposition will be less vigorous. We see a similar phenomenon in the health care arena, where many industries that opposed efforts at reform in the 1990s now at least recognize the problem and have lined up behind the general concept of reform—although no consensus has yet been reached on a solution.

---

[1] The tax code could be used to provide an incentive for participation in a job sharing scheme. In the previous chapter I suggested the idea of "progressive" deductions for wages paid. In a similar fashion, higher deductions could be provided to businesses that agreed to incorporate job sharing into their business models.

One thing that is abundantly clear is that, in a world where traditional jobs are disappearing, access to health care insurance cannot be coupled to employment. One of the primary near term goals for the United States should be to establish a universal health care system that is not tied to jobs. Additionally, as I pointed out in Chapter 3, payroll taxes will become increasingly unsustainable. The first steps in transitioning to a new model will have to be to shift the burden for maintaining social programs away from taxes on individual jobs and toward a broader, more sustainable model which falls more fairly on capital intensive industries that employ relatively few people. The burden that falls on a business should depend not on how many workers it employs, but on how successful that business is at deriving wealth from the market.

Once a system is put in place that allows work to be shared on an equitable basis, it should be possible to achieve a relatively smooth transition into an automated economy. Over time, the incentive-based income streams provided by the government would increase, and the amount of traditional work performed would decrease. As job automation increases and the wages paid by businesses fall, the special taxes that have been put in place would need to be gradually increased to recapture the income.

In addition to the primary economic objective of sustaining consumer demand, this would of course, have many positive impacts on society. Individuals would have more time for family, leisure, personal health and education. Better educated consumers with more leisure time and more confidence in their future incomes would result in sustained consumer spending, vibrant demand for new products and services, and long-term economic growth. As incentive-based income became more important relative to traditional wages, individuals would see increasingly potent incentives to act in environmentally conscious ways, and that would potentially have a significant, favorable impact on climate change and other environmental challenges in the coming decades.

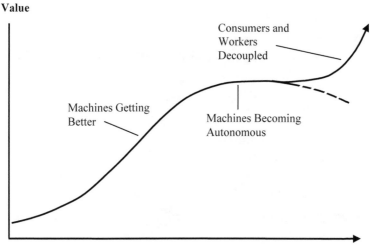

Transitional Economy

Average Income

Keynesian Grandchildren

While few contemporary economists seem particularly concerned about the seemingly inevitable transition to an automated economy, one legendary economist did have remarkable insight into the future. In 1930, as the world plunged into the Great Depression, John Maynard Keynes wrote an essay entitled "Economic Possibilities for our Grandchildren."[53] In his essay, Keynes coined the term "technological unemployment," writing:

> We are being inflicted with a new disease of which some readers many not yet have heard the name, but of which they will hear a great deal in the years to come—namely, *technological unemployment.* This means unemployment due to our discovery of means of economising the use of labour outrunning the pace at which we can find new uses for labour.[']

Keynes recognized that, in 1930, technological unemployment would be a temporary phenomenon and that the economy would eventually absorb the excess workers. The main thrust of his essay was to attempt to look much fur-

---

['] Today, when economists discuss the causes of the Great Depression, they tend to focus almost exclusively on the monetary policy of the Federal Reserve. While there is little doubt that the overly restrictive policies of the Fed prolonged the Depression and perhaps turned a run of the mill recession into a disaster, it should not be forgotten that there was a widespread belief at the time that the technological unemployment (and the resulting plunge in consumer demand) that Keynes spoke of played an important role. Even Albert Einstein expressed this opinion when asked for his take on the causes of the Depression during a visit to the United States in 1933.

ther into the future. Keynes argued that over the next hundred years (in other words, by the year 2030), the economies of developed nations would grow dramatically. He showed that, over time, economic growth would operate much like compound interest in a bank account and make the society of the future far more wealthy. Keynes had a very optimistic view of the long-term future; some would argue he was unrealistic. He believed that humanity was "solving its economic problem" and that the future would be one of relative abundance.

Keynes also foresaw clearly that future technologies would result in less need for human labor. He believed that we would enter a new "age of leisure" and he worried that we might struggle to find purpose in a world that did not require work. Importantly, he also foresaw the need to share whatever work was required across the population:

> …we shall endeavor to spread the bread thin on the butter—to make what work there is still to be done to be as widely shared as possible. Three-hour shifts or a fifteen hour work week may put off the problem [the "problem" being a lack or purpose or activity to occupy time] for a great while.

In evaluating Keynes' essay, we should keep in mind that attempting to predict events a hundred years into the future is a remarkably ambitious undertaking. What economist (or stock market trader) today is capable of predicting the status of the economy even six months out with any confidence? Personally, I think that Keynes' take on the future was in many ways remarkably prescient. In particular, I think his view that technological progress would be relentless and would ultimately reduce the need for human labor is very likely to be vindicated in the coming years and decades. His view of how we would go about sharing the work is also essentially correct, but a bit more problematic in terms of how it will evolve. As a practical matter, I think there are a few observations we can make.

First, left to its own devices, the free market is very unlikely to produce a viable system in which work is shared equitably. Employing (and training) multiple people to perform a job that could instead be done by one person places an excess burden on businesses. They will not take on that burden voluntarily. Government regulation will be required to make it happen. Where businesses do today hire part time workers, they often do so in an effort to avoid regulation or paying for benefits. A second obvious problem is that the wages from part time work will not provide anything approaching an adequate income for workers. In today's economy, part time workers often have to string together multiple jobs in order to earn a living wage.

In general, I think three basic things will be required for us to move to an effective transitional economy and to begin to realize the vision that Keynes wrote of in 1930: (1) We will need the government to enforce a work-sharing scheme. (2) We need to decouple health care and other social safety nets from employment, and (3) We need to supplement employment income with direct income streams—and I have argued strongly that these income streams should be unequal and based on incentives.

These incentives—particularly a focus on continuing education—will offer at least a partial solution to the problems of a lack of purpose and an excess of free time that Keynes foresaw.

Transition in the Tunnel

Let's now return to our tunnel and rewind the simulation to the point at which automation starts to take hold. We can then see how our transitional strategy might work.

* * * * *

We are back in our tunnel. Very gradually, just as before, we begin to automate the jobs held by many of the average lights. As this happens, the impacted lights grow dimmer and in many cases disappear completely.

Now, however, we notice something new in the tunnel. A *green* light has appeared. As we watch closely, we see that many more lights gradually begin to shift in hue. The intensity of the lights remains unchanged, but the color rotates between white and green. Some lights rotate rapidly between green and white light, while others shift their color much more slowly.

The green light, of course, represents the purchasing power of consumers who are supported by incentive-based income streams rather than traditional jobs. The lights rotate in color as jobs are shared among the workers first affected by automation.

The green lights initially represent a small minority of the lights within the tunnel. Most people continue to be employed in traditional jobs. If we were to watch the action in the tunnel over time, however, we would see that the number of green lights is constantly increasing. Likewise, if we were to focus on any one light, we would see that, as it rotates between white and green, the green light gradually comes to predominate.

While the color rotation among the lights captures our interest for a time, the most striking realization is that nothing else has changed in the tunnel. As we watch, we see that the lights continue to softly impact the panels on the walls of the tunnel as consumers purchase products and services. The businesses in the tunnel make no distinctions based on the color of the lights. Over time, the process of creative destruction continues just as it always has. Inefficient businesses fail and new ones rise up to take their place.

Among the multitude of lights in the tunnel, we can see that there are still a significant minority which shine with intense white light. The wealthiest people in the tunnel may be subject to somewhat higher tax rates, but the businesses and assets they own are retaining their value as the mass market continues to thrive.

Overall, we sense that stability has returned to the tunnel. As the collective light that permeates the tunnel gradually shifts from white to green, we can also sense that it is once again increasing in overall intensity. Even as jobs are relentlessly automated away, the logic of the free market has been successfully leveraged to once again drive sustained prosperity.

Chapter 5

THE GREEN LIGHT

In the previous chapter, I proposed a mechanism for adapting the market economy so that it can continue to function even as machine automation inexorably eliminates the jobs that provide income to consumers. The essential idea is that we should impose some combination of a consumption tax and/or a special direct tax on business that captures the income which, in a non-automated economy, would be paid out in wages. Over time, as the wages paid to average workers decrease (as a percentage of revenue), these taxes would be gradually increased to recapture at least a portion of this income. The overall objective is to recapture just the optimal amount of income and then get it into the hands of consumers so that there will be sufficient consumer demand to continue driving the economy.

Once the income has been collected, I then argued that it should be directed to individual consumers based on incentives. If, in the future, most human labor will someday be unnecessary, then it follows that the private sector will not be willing to pay for it. If we cannot pay people to work, then we must pay them to do something else that has value. As I pointed out in the previous chapter, we can construct a number of incentives which will drive people to act in ways that benefit themselves and society, and which help to protect the environment. By offering unequal incentive-based income to consumers, we not only sustain consumer demand, but also drive people to act in ways that benefit us all and provide each person with the possibility of advancement and a higher income in the future.

This hope for the future—the idea that by striving to complete goals one can attain a better standard of living—is critical to both individual and collective stability. It offers a way to avoid the enormous problem of an ever increasing, impoverished, disenfranchised and unmotivated underclass. As we saw, the incentive-based income scheme can be combined with a job rotation or sharing plan so that as automation progresses, the remaining work is shared on a reasonably equitable basis among the population.

In this chapter, we are going to use some imagination and push forward even further into the future. Let's suppose that our transition has been underway for some time in the major industrialized and emerging economies. Things have progressed to the point where the majority of people in the developed world no longer work full time. Most consumers now receive a substantial portion of their income from incentive-based income streams. Based on their particular interests and abilities, people pursue higher education, work in the community and make choices that benefit the environment with the understanding that doing these things will lead to a higher income and a better standard of living. Average people have sufficient income, and sufficient confidence in the future, so that both consumer spending and overall economic activity consistently grow over time.

While most people work only part time, or in some cases not at all, a significant minority continues to pursue a full time career. Some may still find employment in specific areas where there continues to be need. Authors, artists, and entertainers will still be accorded the opportunity to derive substantial income from their talents. And, of course, there are still people who have the necessary skills and ability to start successful businesses and engage directly in innovation. Because the transition has successfully preserved a robust consumer market, those with the appropriate talent and ambition still have the potential to become wealthy. In fact, it is likely that much of the traditional work now performed by people is entrepreneurial in nature. Many people may choose to engage in profitable hobbies or part time businesses that augment their income.

Prosperity has been preserved in the developed and emerging economies. Our next task is to think about how this new system might be extended to the poorest regions of the world.

Attacking Poverty

Most of us understand that there is a basic inequity in the fact that the vast majority of the world's wealth resides with a relatively small fraction of its population, and we realize that this inequality is an important factor that often underlies conflict, terrorism, and general political instability. Economists have tried for decades to come up with strategies that might help developing nations climb the ladder of prosperity. Relatively few of these efforts have achieved any substantial degree of success.

Partly, the reason is that figuring out how to invest in a developing country in such a way as to ensure that the investment results in sustained growth is extraordinarily difficult. A common problem is, of course, corruption among officials in the country. These people very often act primarily for their own benefit—and, in particular, in ways that preserve their positions and power—rather than for the benefit of their country as a whole. In the final analysis, it comes down to individual incentives. People are primarily motivated to do things that they are paid to do. Making an arms length investment in a country and somehow insuring that that investment creates appropriate and sustainable incentives throughout the economy is an extraordinary challenge.[54]

A second issue we face in confronting poverty is the environmental impact that it implies. If we look at a rapidly developing county, such as China, it quickly becomes apparent that addressing poverty by applying the normal, historical path to industrialization throughout the poorest regions of the world could well result in global catastrophe. The earth is simply not equipped to support untold billions of people who begin to utilize energy and other resources at levels typical for the major industrialized economies.

In this chapter, I am going to argue that, in a largely automated economy, it should be possible to attack poverty simply by gradually extending incentive-based incomes to people in developing countries. The payments would start out relatively low and the incentives would strongly emphasize environmental considerations. By paying people directly to conserve resources and protect the environment, it should be possible to move toward decoupling economic prosperity from negative ecological impact.

Clearly, such an initiative would require a high degree of international cooperation and probably the formation of an agency that would impose standards and help design income incentives for individual countries. It is possible that some governments would initially refuse to participate. Over time, however, if the approach proved successful, it seems likely that the populations of nearly every country would demand participation.

Once again, we are likely to run into the "paying people for nothing" psychological stumbling block. The initial reaction of many people would probably be that such a scheme would be highly inflationary. To see that this would not necessarily be the case, let's start with a somewhat simplistic analysis of why such a scheme would *not* work in our current economy.

Imagine that, in today's world, we simply started providing incomes to large numbers of impoverished people throughout the world. We might borrow the money for this, or simply have governments print it. Once the money found its way into the hands of these people, they would, of course, start to spend it. Businesses both locally and in other countries would try to ramp up to meet this new demand. They would have to find and hire workers for this. We can easily imagine that shortages of skilled workers might develop and that wages would therefore increase. In short, the economy's ability to produce real goods and services would not be able to keep up with all the new money now in the hands of consumers. The result, of course, would be inflation: the value of all this new money would fall, and prices and interest rates would increase, perhaps dramatically.

But what if the entire economy were highly automated? Then, no new workers would need to be hired, and there would be few if any labor shortages. There would be a need for additional capital investment in technology to meet the new demand, but this would be a good investment that would continue to pay off over the long term. We cannot say that all the constraints that might lead to inflation would be removed because there might still be shortages of energy or resources. However, such shortages are not specific to this approach—in other words, if we attempted to address poverty by the traditional method of building up industry and creating jobs, natural resource and energy constraints would still come into play.

Money has value only because it can be exchanged for real products and services. In our current economy, it takes a great deal of human labor to produce those products and services. Therefore, it is fair to say that the value of money is tied very closely to productivity, or the general efficiency of production. If in fact, the economy of the future is highly automated and requires few workers, then we can imagine that it may well be possible to achieve a level of economic efficiency that is far beyond what is possible today.[ ] Furthermore, an automated economy seems likely to be highly scalable: in other words, it would be much easier to rapidly and smoothly ramp up production in order to meet increased demand.

I believe that it may someday be possible to leverage the vastly increased production efficiency of an automated economy to address the issue of global poverty. As long as incomes were provided in a gradual fashion so that any inflationary effects could be controlled, and as long as individual incomes were tied to incentives that helped address environmental impact and resource constraints, it should conceptually be possible to eventually eliminate poverty. Additionally, I think it may be possible to create a "virtuous cycle" in which billions of newly viable consumers would eventually drive global economic output to unimaginable levels by creating markets of staggering size for new products and services.

Many people will, of course, feel that all this is pure fantasy. Obviously, this is not an idea that is going to be feasible in the near future, and it clearly could not occur at

---

[ ] Additionally, we can speculate that if production efficiency reached unprecedented heights as automation invaded the economy, we would also need a much more relaxed monetary policy than is currently the case. Central banks would probably have to allow the money supply to expand at a rapid rate relative to historical norms, or production would be needlessly constrained. This is a very strong argument against the idea (as proposed by some extreme Libertarians) that we should return to the gold standard.

all if we don't find a way to navigate through the transition that I discussed in the previous chapter. Nonetheless, I would argue that this lies within the realm of future possibility—perhaps even by our cutoff date of 2089. To flesh this idea out a little further, let's use even more imagination and consider the possible economic implications of truly advanced technologies that might conceivably be available in the distant future.

Fundamental Economic Constraints

Given the fact that we have billions of people who all desire material things, why doesn't global economic output simply soar toward infinity? Obviously, there are things that limit production. Let's make a list of the most basic factors that act to constrain economic activity:

1. Labor

In today's economy, human labor is required to some degree in the production of nearly everything. The availability of workers, the cost of employing them and the specific skills that they possess is an important constraint on economic output. Obviously, the point of this book has been that this constraint is likely to become far less important as automation technology progresses.

2. Energy, Land, Natural Resources and Environmental Impact

Clearly, production is constrained by the availability of energy and of the raw materials, suitable land, water, and other resources that are required to create products and services. Additionally, economic activity will ultimately be limited by the harmful effects it perpetrates on the environment: including toxic pollution, over use of public resources, and, of course, the climate change effects associated with the emission of carbon dioxide and other greenhouse gasses.

3. Technology

Production is also limited by the sophistication of the machines, processes and techniques that are available. I have argued here that, as technology advances, it will ultimately become independent of labor. Machines will evolve to the point where they are no longer tools used by workers, but instead autonomous producers.

4. Consumer Demand

Viable consumer demand is also an absolute limiter of production in the free market economy. We are, of course, speaking here of demand in the economic sense, which means desire for a product or service combined with the ability and willingness to pay for it. No business will invest in production unless there is either existing market demand or the reasonable expectation of such demand in the foreseeable future. The idea that production responds to demand is one of the defining characteristics of capitalism.

Removing the Constraints

Now that we've listed the four basic constraints on production let's perform a thought experiment and imagine how those constraints might conceivably fall in the distant future if technology continues to relentlessly advance. The point is simply to imagine which constraints could potentially be eliminated or minimized as technology progresses over decades and even centuries.

The main thesis of this book has been that, eventually, machines will become autonomous and there will be far less need for human labor. Therefore, let's go ahead and remove labor as a constraint. Our list now looks like this:

1. Energy, Land, Natural Resources and Environmental Impact

2. Technology

3. Consumer Demand

Next, let's imagine that advanced nanotechnology and new clean energy technologies become available. Perhaps we manage to derive nearly limitless energy from the sun or from nuclear fusion. The cost of energy, as well as its negative impact on the environment, fall to a near zero level. Nanotechnology allows us to easily transform matter at the molecular level. We can inexpensively construct advanced materials from more basic components and recycle used and waste products into usable raw materials. Environmental policies and incentives have effectively minimized other negative impacts that result from production.

We can then reduce our list of economic constraints as follows:

1. Technology

2. Consumer Demand

Now imagine that, in the absence of resource constraints, technology continues its relentless advance and ultimately accelerates to the point where new processes and machines can be conceived and constructed almost effortlessly. Technology, much like energy, becomes universally available and virtually free.

Our list can now be reduced to a single line:

1. Consumer Demand

And now we must stop. Consumer demand as a constraint is fundamental to the architecture of the free market system. If we eliminate this constraint—if production occurs in response to something other than demand from consumers who have the ability to pay for the products and services produced—then we no longer have a market economy.

Obviously, this exercise has been purely imaginary. While it might be centuries before technology advances sufficiently to actually remove these constraints, we can reasonably expect that, over time, technology will gradually act to reduce them. By thinking about which constraints could possibly be eliminated far in the future, we can begin to see what is truly important. Each of the constraints could conceivably be reduced, or perhaps even eliminated, *except consumer demand.*

The Evolution toward Consumption

Historically, the primary economic contribution of an individual has been his or her work. Our economic rules emphasize production because prosperity has always been heavily dependent on human labor. The incentives built into the market economy reflect this historical reality.

Consumption is seen as a privilege that derives from our participation in production. As we can see from the thought experiment we just conducted, however, in the long run it is really *consumption*—not production—that is the one human economic contribution that will always be indispensable.

If we are to fully leverage the production potential of the advanced technologies that will become available in the decades and centuries ahead, I believe we will have to re-engineer our economic system so that consumption is largely decoupled from individual participation in production. Consumption, rather than production, will eventually have to become the primary economic contribution made by the bulk of average people. If we fail to make this adaptation, technological advance is likely to ultimately be self-limiting, and may well lead to decline rather than increased prosperity.[1] If, however, we succeed in evolving to a system that sustains vibrant consumer demand even as accelerating technology drives back other economic constraints, we may conceivably emerge into a new era of unprecedented economic growth and prosperity.

I have argued in this book that consumers should eventually be provided with income based on incentives. Currently, people are offered incentives to contribute directly to overall prosperity through work. In the future, we should instead offer people incentives to behave in ways that *do not detract* from the prosperity that will result from increasingly automated production. As individuals act according to these incentives, they will earn the income they

---

[1] Please see the "Technology Paradox" in the Appendix.

require to participate as consumers in the market economy.

The idea that an individual's consumption might someday be valued above his or her contribution to production is very difficult to accept. It flies directly in the face of the values and the work ethic that are instilled in the vast majority of us. Undoubtedly, it will take time to adapt to this new reality.

I think it is probably fair to say that, for the majority of the population, the specific job a person happens to perform does not meaningfully capture his or her uniqueness as a human being. While a minority of lucky individuals may have careers that fully engage and even define them, most average people probably work at their current jobs primarily because they have few other choices. For most of us, our job is really not who we are.

But what about our consumption? If you could record in time and place every purchase made by an individual during the course of a lifetime, surely you would end up with something unique. A record that would reflect in some way almost every aspect of a person's arc through life—virtually an economic DNA sequence. Consumption is by far the best overall economic gauge of who we really are. And yet, these routine, daily purchasing decisions are amplified by the mechanism of the market into a force that creates and destroys entire industries. Collective consumer choices have provided the basic logic that has disciplined and directed markets—and therefore driven technological progress—for centuries. In a very real sense, the specific choices we make as consumers create our overall prosperity. This is why capitalism has succeeded, and other economic systems have failed.

In time, I think it is likely that our perceptions will shift so that we begin to truly recognize the economic contribution that our individual marketplace decisions make. Someday, the majority of people will be valued in economic terms not for what they directly produce, but for their participation in consumption markets. If we can succeed in gradually extending that participation to the billions of people who are now trapped in poverty—and do so in a way that creates incentives to conserve resources and minimize environmental impact—we may find that the resulting consumer demand is capable of fueling an engine that can drive us to unprecedented economic heights.

The Green Light

The natural cycle in the tunnel is stable and reinforcing. The vast majority of the consumers in the tunnel now glow with a predominantly green light. As time passes, the collective intensity of the lights continues to gradually increase.

Suddenly, we see that vast numbers of dim green lights have begun to stream into the tunnel. These new lights have barely enough intensity to make it past the threshold, but once inside, they join the river of lights as it courses over the panels on the tunnel walls. At first, we sense that the businesses in the tunnel are straining somewhat to meet this new demand, but as time passes, the cycle again strengthens. The collective intensity of the light in the tunnel begins to quickly increase. We also notice that, over time, each of the new dim lights is very gradually becoming brighter.

As the new lights stream into the tunnel and are incorporated into its natural cycle, we see that some bright white lights begin to pulse with new energy. New panels are now appearing in many places on the tunnel walls that were once dark. The entrepreneurs and business owners in the tunnel are responding to the rapidly increasing demand.

As the number of lights continues to increase, the speed with which panels are updated and the number of new panels appearing on the tunnel walls seems to accelerate. Although we had perceived the tunnel as being almost infinitely vast, it now appears that the walls are completely covered with panels.

Even as we sense this, however, the tunnel itself begins to expand. As new panels rapidly fill the spaces on the expanding tunnel walls, we notice that some of the brightest white lights are now radiating with an unprecedented intensity. Still, as the ever-increasing cycle of light continues to parade through the expanding tunnel, we sense strongly that it is the seemingly infinite number of green lights that truly encapsulates the collective energy, enterprise and hope of all human beings.

APPENDIX / FINAL THOUGHTS

Are the ideas presented in this book WRONG? (Opposing arguments with responses)

In this section I have listed some of the arguments that may be made against the ideas in this book, together with my responses. These are either conventional arguments or things I have thought of or seen elsewhere.

The economy will always create new jobs; we will never have structural unemployment as a result of advancing technology

This is the idea behind the "Luddite fallacy" which I discussed at some length in Chapters 2 and 3 (see pages 95 and 131). At present, I suspect that most economists would probably be likely to agree with this statement and, therefore, disagree with what I have suggested in this book. Here, in a nutshell, is my argument for why I think we *will* end up with a serious unemployment problem:

As technology advances and industries automate, this improves the efficiency of production and tends to make the products and services produced by those industries more affordable. That leaves more purchasing power in the pockets of consumers. Those consumers then go out and spend that extra money on all kinds of products and services produced by a variety of industries. Some of those industries are relatively labor intensive, so they have to hire more workers to meet this demand—and so overall employment remains stable or increases. This is the reason that, historically, technology has not led to sustained, widespread unemployment.

My argument is that accelerating automation technology will ultimately invade many of the industries that have traditionally been labor intensive. Additionally, the process of creative destruction will destroy old industries and create new ones, and very few of these new industries are likely to be labor intensive. As a result, the overall economy will become less labor intensive and ultimately reach a "tipping point." Beyond this point, the economy will no longer be able to absorb the workers who lose jobs due to automation: businesses will instead invest primarily in more machines. I have also argued that this process will be relentless, and if it is not addressed by some type of government policy, we may ultimately see a precipitous drop in consumer spending as a substantial fraction of the population loses confidence in its future income continuity. That, of course, would result in even more unemployment and a downward spiral would ensue.

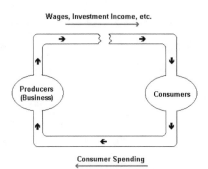

If technology resulted in unemployment, everyone would already be out of a job because technological progress has been going on for hundreds of years

This really just amounts to saying "it hasn't happened yet, so it will never happen." History has proven time and again that, where technology is concerned, something can be impossible since the dawn of civilization and then suddenly, in the blink of an eye, become *possible*. Revolutionary technologies, such as the airplane and nuclear power, were all dismissed as being impossible even by preeminent scientists who were involved in the research that led to their development.

Today, most of us accept that technology will continue to advance and produce *things* that we might currently view as impossible. However, we still think too narrowly. We accept that there will be new technologies, new products and new industries, but most of us are not prepared to accept that all this will change the basic economic rules that we take for granted. But why wouldn't that be the case? Is there a fundamental reason why accelerating technology should impact nearly every aspect of our lives—but *not* impact the way the economy works? As I pointed out in Chapter 2, advancing information technology—because it enabled the creation and distribution of financial derivatives—has certainly played an important role in the severity of the current economic crisis. I suspect that this is just a preview of the economic impacts that technology will have in the future.

The population is aging. Once the baby boomers retire, we will have a worker shortage—not unemployment

In nearly all the developed nations (and also in China), the populations are rapidly aging and retirement plans are projected to come under intense pressure, as too few young workers have to support too many older retired people. Does this imply that there is likely to be an overall shortage of workers as large numbers of older people leave the workforce? I think it is certainly possible this may be a counteractive force that might tend to delay the impact from automation to a certain extent. Here are some things to consider:

- The impact of automation on a specific job category is really not related to the number of workers available to perform that type of job. Once technology advances to the point where a type of job can be automated, the machines to do this can easily be replicated. Machines do not need to be educated or trained, and so they are not subject to the bottlenecks that create shortages of workers in fields such as nursing. Therefore, in considering the overall impact of machine automation, the important criterion is not the number of workers available but the *types* of jobs that can be automated. To the extent that there are worker shortages within a specific job category, that would actually tend to increase the incentive for automation technologies to be developed in that area. We already see this effect in Japan where significant work is being done to develop robots capable of assisting with care of the elderly population.

- The current consensus view seems to be that, as a result of the 2008-9 financial crisis (and its impact on 401k plans), many workers will remain in the workforce longer than originally planned. This will give automation technology longer to come into play before any worker shortages materialize.

- Even if the aging population does tend to retard unemployment, this would, of course, simply be a delaying factor—not a long-term solution to the problem.

I think we can certainly expect to see worker shortages in some areas, but this may very possibly be combined with an overall unemployment problem. The danger is that increasing structural unemployment will unfold in parallel with the demographic problem. I suspect that most of the projections regarding the impact of aging populations assume reasonably full employment among younger workers. If this does not turn out to be the case, the situation will obviously be much worse. As I pointed out in Chapter 3, a payroll tax-based system for supporting retirement programs might become completely unsustainable.

Businesses will never fully automate because of the high initial capital investment and the lack of flexibility this implies

There are some valid points here, and I think that these factors may, in many cases, serve to retard the process of automation—but in the long run they will not prevent it. Some businesses will certainly delay automation because of the high capital outlays required. However, over time, machines will become more affordable, more reliable, and more flexible. At some point, as technology advances, machines will begin to outperform workers to the extent that a non-automated business will not be competitive. Consider the case of online banking: it generally offers a range of services, such as automatic bill paying, that could not be offered by a human bank teller.

Keep in mind that automation offers cost benefits beyond simply eliminating wages. There are also payroll taxes, benefits, vacation time, management issues (and if you eliminate workers, you can in many cases also get rid of the first line managers), etc. There are also safety and liability issues; consider the safety advantages of a fully automated warehouse.

The need for technical and economic flexibility may also tend to hold back automation for a time. If a business invests heavily in specific machines to produce a particular product and then that product does not sell well, it may be stuck with equipment it does not want. The obvious answer to that is that, in the future, automation technology will be more flexible and easy to adapt to different products. I think the manufacturers of automation equipment are fully aware of this issue and will build increasingly flexible products.

There is also the issue of economic flexibility: a business that employs workers can lay them off in slow times, while a more automated business will be stuck with its machines. Again, I think that, in the long run, as technology advances, businesses that don't automate will simply not be able to compete: and that reality will overwhelm other considerations.

Another point is that both of these factors (high capital costs and the need for flexibility) may tend to push the next wave of automation toward software applications geared toward eliminating knowledge worker jobs. Software is typically more flexible and has a lower up front cost than expensive mechanical automation. As I noted in Chapter 2, automation of these jobs, together with offshoring, may mean diminishing prospects for knowledge works and college graduates in general.

Machines may take over most unskilled labor, but they will never be able to do skilled or professional jobs that require lots of training and education

I think this is a dangerous misconception that stems, in part, from a certain amount of hubris on the part of people who are well educated. The conventional wisdom is that a fence has been erected within our society. On the lush, garden side of the fence, are workers who have strong educations and training. These people are beneficiaries of the information age. On the toxic wasteland side of the fence, are relatively unskilled workers. These people have been heavily impacted by both technology and glob-alization. They often survive by stringing two or three part time jobs together or work in low wage jobs with few ben-efits. The obvious solution is for us to find a way to offer these people additional training—so they can hop over to the good side of the fence.

I think that the problem with this scenario is that *the fence is going to move*, and it may move very rapidly. The good side of the fence is going to contract, and increasing num-bers of well-educated workers are going to find themselves suddenly on the toxic side. As I pointed out in Chapter 2, we can expect fields such as artificial intelligence to ad-vance rapidly in the coming years and decades. While many college-educated knowledge workers perform tasks that are currently beyond the capability of computers, they nonetheless have jobs that can be broken down into a rela-tively narrow set of tasks and routines. Over time, these jobs will be increasingly subject to automation, and may well come under significant pressure from offshoring even sooner. As this trend develops, I think that the psycholog-ical impact on consumers will represent a significant dan-ger to the economy.

Even if I am wrong and increasing unemployment is confined primarily to lower skill workers, the overall im-pact on our society and economy would be dramatically negative. In the United States, two thirds of workers—and therefore consumers—do not have a college degree. While efforts to improve education and training are laudable, the reality is that this is not likely to offset the impact of geo-metrically accelerating technology. In fact, I think that the arguments I have put forth in this book remain relevant even in the (I think unlikely) event that more educated workers are spared the impact of automation.

A great many jobs require "people skills" and, therefore, could not be performed by machines

I think there are definitely some jobs that meet this standard, but probably not anywhere near enough to avoid the overall problem that would result from automation. I also think that people often tend to underestimate the extent to which their job might be susceptible to automation. Bank tellers have "people" jobs, but that has not stopped people from using ATMs or online banking. In general, consumers seem quite receptive to automation and self-service technologies if they provide convenience.

Many workers whose interactions with other people are primarily internal to their organization might feel that they have jobs in which people skills are critical. If you think about it, however, that is true only if most of the *other jobs* are also being done by people. Once automation takes hold within an organization, such people skills might eventually be far less important.

Finally, it is important to note that automation will have both a direct and an indirect impact on jobs. Even a person who holds a job that is completely safe from automation might still be impacted by declining consumer demand resulting from jobs elsewhere in the economy being automated.

Perhaps machines will ultimately take over most of the work done by people, but this won't happen until far into the future (hundreds of years, etc.)

In general, if my argument here turns out to not be correct, then there are really two basic ways in which it can be wrong:

- The argument could be fundamentally wrong. This implies that the economy is capable of growing and advancing technologically basically *forever*, without creating an unemployment problem. In other words, even 500 years from now, when society presumably has technology that is incomprehensible to us today, the economy will still provide employment for the vast majority of people in the population.

- The argument could be premature. Maybe the ideas here are basically correct, but they won't come into play until far into the future. However, once we acknowledge that at some point in the future, the economy may become nearly fully automated, then as a matter of mathematics, we cannot get to that point without first passing through a tipping point—beyond which structural unemployment will begin to be a problem. The tipping point could occur long before we expect it.

I would guess that if the trends I have presented here do not develop, then it will most likely be because I have gotten the timing wrong. However, I do think there is some pretty compelling evidence that we are fairly close to the point where accelerating machine capability is going to have a dramatic economic impact (if we have not already passed that point). Please see the section "Where are we now? Four Possible Cases" later in the Appendix for more on this.

In the future, wages/income may be very low because of job automation, but technology will also make everything plentiful and cheap—so low income won't matter

This is an idea that is often expressed in conjunction with a discussion of advanced nanotechnology. Nanotechnology may one day offer the promise of material objects constructed molecule-by-molecule, perhaps using self-replicating technologies. Some people argue that, taken to the extreme, this might mean that physical objects could be constructed in a way that is analogous to the creation of virtual objects displayed on a computer screen (think of the "replicator" in *Star Trek*). There are, of course, a few problems with this:

- Expenditures on manufactured goods represent a fairly small percentage of the average consumer's spending. Expenses like housing[1] and health care are far

---

[1] It is perhaps conceivable that job automation may someday lead to somewhat lower housing costs because it could result in a lot of empty office towers and commercial buildings. Those buildings might then be converted to other uses—including perhaps housing. If knowledge worker and office jobs migrate into the computer network, the really hot commercial real estate in the future might be in the locations where companies like Google and Microsoft are now building huge

more important. So even if the price of most goods fell dramatically, consumers would still need an adequate income.

- Today, we already have digital products that have a zero marginal cost of production. These products are, for the most part, not free because they have intellectual property rights attached to them. We can expect the same if advanced nanotechnology arrives someday. If there isn't a way to protect and profit from these property rights, it is very unlikely that investors would provide the enormous sums necessary to realize the technology.

- Advanced nanotechnology almost certainly lies further in the future than the automation technology that is likely to threaten routine jobs. So it won't arrive in time to solve the problem in any case.

The "Heads in the Sand" Objection

If other arguments against the ideas I have presented here prove insufficient, then I suspect that many people will be tempted to turn to this one:

Some people will reject the idea that machines might begin to exhibit some degree of intelligence—and, therefore, achieve the capability to perform a great many jobs—simply because the implications are very difficult to deal with. This irrational, but perhaps understandable, objec-

---

"server farms." These are usually relatively isolated locations far from natural disasters and other threats and close to clean, reliable energy (which today mostly means hydroelectric power).

tion to the idea that machines might someday begin to think and reason was first articulated by the founder of computer science, Alan Turing (Please see the last section of this Appendix).

Turing initiated the field of artificial intelligence with his 1950 paper "Computing Machinery and Intelligence." Here's how Turing expressed what he called the "Heads in the Sand" Objection (which, of course, he rejected):

"The consequences of machines thinking would be too dreadful. Let us hope and believe that they cannot do so." [55]

Two Questions Worth Thinking About

One

While you might not agree that it will ever be a reality, it is easy to *imagine* an economy with no human workers. Obviously if autonomous machines could do everything, people could spend their time doing whatever they liked.

Can you imagine a market economy with no *consumers?*

Two

Most economists would probably agree that long-term economic growth and prosperity (perhaps as measured by growth in per capita GDP) is tied pretty closely to technological progress. This is the same as saying that society becomes more wealthy largely because the machines we use to produce goods and services get better over time. We all assume that economic growth can continue indefinitely. This implies that machines will have to continue getting better basically forever.

Can a machine keep getting better *forever* without someday becoming autonomous?

Where are we now? Four Possible Cases

On the next page, I've reproduced the scary graph from Chapter 3, which shows the potential impact of machines throughout the economy becoming more autonomous. Remember that this graph shows average income for a "median range" of people in the economy; it's based on what statisticians would call a "truncated mean" with the poorest and wealthiest people removed before calculating the average. The reason for doing this is that we know automation will tend to concentrate income and perhaps drag up overall average income—at least for a while. Ultimately however, the collective impact on the bulk of consumers will become overwhelming, and a graph of per capita GDP should have a similar shape.

If the basic shape of this graph is correct, then the real question is: where are we on the graph now? I think there are four possible cases, as shown on the diagram. Keep in mind that while the graph I have drawn is smooth to show the general trend, in reality the graph would likely have many short-term ups and downs. This will make it very difficult to figure out where we are.

Value Added (Wage) of Average Worker Operating Average Machine

Also: Overall Wealth of Society (GDP per capita will look similar)

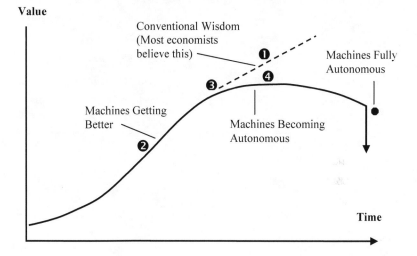

1. If the ideas I've presented in this book are wrong, then the conventional wisdom is correct, and the current crisis is just an aberration. We should eventually get back on track and continue climbing the graph.

2. If the shape of the graph is basically correct, but we are still far away from the point where automation is going to become important, then we should, likewise, get back on track and continue climbing.

3. If we are somewhere close to the point where the dotted and solid lines diverge, then we are going to see increasing economic impacts, and we will have difficulty in achieving sustained, long-term growth. If I had to bet, I would choose this case.

4. If things have gotten away from us, then we could, in fact, be much further along than we imagine. This could perhaps be explained by suggesting that consumer borrowing masked the reality of the situation over the last few years and that the current crisis is the beginning of the reckoning. This is an ugly scenario, but I don't think it can be dismissed completely. Obviously, if this is the case, we need to adopt new policies rapidly.

The Next 10-20 years: Some Indicators to Watch For

The ideas that I have presented in this book might be said to constitute a hypothesis, or perhaps a theory that is still lacking in substantial supporting evidence. This book is obviously not based on an analysis of historical economic data, but rather on a rational, and I think somewhat conservative, projection of existing trends in information technology. Nonetheless, I believe that there is already at least some empirical evidence to support this hypothesis.

I cannot reasonably expect anyone to accept these ideas on the basis of what is presented here alone. My intent in writing this book has been to try to raise the general level of awareness regarding this issue. My hope is that economists and others may begin to look for evidence of the trend toward an automated economy with an open mind, so that we will have a reasonable chance of addressing the risks we may face in the future. Toward that end, here are some general indicators that I think may constitute reasonable evidence that we are moving along the path I have sketched out here.

Weak consumer spending pushes investment toward cost cutting and labor saving technologies

Nearly everyone seems to be projecting that when recovery from the current downturn comes, it will be relatively weak. Economists are once again anticipating a "jobless recovery." (When is the last time we had a recovery that *wasn't* jobless?) In the face of lingering unemployment and tight credit, consumer demand in the United States is almost certain to be unimpressive for some time. The wind has been knocked out of the world economy's primary consumption engine, and it remains unclear where sustainable future demand will come from. I've seen several articles in the financial press that point out that our future prosperity will likely depend on us consuming less and exporting more. Yes, but *who* is going to buy all those exports?

If projections for consumer spending remain unoptimistic, many businesses are likely to hold back on general technology investment as they wait for a more sustainable recovery. As a result, we may continue to see relatively low levels of venture capital flowing into start-up firms for some time. In the midst of this, it may become evident that one of the few bright spots is the market for new technology products that result in immediate cost savings. We might see venture capital increasingly begin to flow to start-up companies that are focused on labor saving technologies such as robotics and artificial intelligence.[1] Some of these new ventures might focus on embedding intelligence into the enterprise software used by large corporations, while others create tools that can be used in small businesses via Internet interfaces. Significant effort is likely to be put into machine learning technology, so that automation algorithms can be easily taught to perform a variety

---

[1] Obviously, even if the current consensus is wrong and we end up with a surprisingly strong rebound, we are still likely to see significant investment in these areas, as well as a much higher level of technology investment in general.

of jobs. Because automating the jobs of relatively unskilled workers often requires high capital investment in mechanically complex machines, it may well be office and knowledge workers who are the primary initial targets of these new technologies.

Offshoring and automation begin to penetrate small business and possibly combine to capture higher value jobs

I suspect that most economists discount the potential for outsourcing to invade the small business arena because they assume that the costs and inconveniences associated with setting up offshore relationships constitute a barrier. My concern is that the offshoring industry, especially if it faces diminished demand in other areas, will move to minimize this barrier by adopting Internet-based interfaces that make it easy for smaller businesses to offshore specific jobs and tasks—without any need to travel or engage in complex negotiations. I think it is likely that exactly the same thing will happen with increasingly sophisticated automation software. If this were to occur, it would eventually undercut the U.S. economy's primary job creation engine to a significant degree.

A second possibility is that as increased investment in artificial intelligence-driven productivity tools begins to bear fruit, these tools may be combined with highly educated, but young and inexpensive, offshore workers to capture jobs which are currently held by highly paid knowledge workers with deep experience. As AI software advances, it will increasingly begin to encapsulate what we think of as "experience" and "judgment" within specific fields of knowledge. An intelligent and educated young worker wielding such tools might eventually be competitive with professionals and workers who currently command very high salaries.

Labor intensive areas of the economy begin to see increased automation

As I have pointed out several times in this book, the primary danger to the U.S. economy will be when labor-intensive industries, especially in the service sector, become susceptible to automation. In areas such as retail and fast food where wages are low, automation may be held at bay for a time by the high capital costs of automation equipment. However, as technology advances and costs fall, I think it is inevitable that at some point, the tradeoff will begin to make sense and competitive pressures will push businesses and industries toward automation.

New technology industries fail to create significant numbers of jobs

We can expect that technological advance will give rise to entirely new industries in the future. However, the reality is that few if any of these are likely to be labor intensive. By their very nature, these new industries will tend to rely on information technology and will offer relatively few opportunities for average workers. There is also a risk that these new industries may directly compete with and ultimately destroy existing, more labor intensive industries.

One exception to this may be the so called "green collar" jobs that involve installing solar panels, wind turbines, and so forth. These, however, are really one-time infrastructure jobs. Alone, they will not be sufficient to provide sustainable employment growth.

Diminishing prospects for college graduates

Unfortunately, as I suggested in Chapter 2, I think there are reasons to expect that the assumption that a college degree is a ticket to success may ultimately be challenged. There are a couple of trends that may develop:

- Unemployment, underemployment and low wages for recent graduates may develop as automation, and possibly offshoring, have a disproportionate impact on entry-level positions. This will be an especially significant problem in light of the enormous debt burdens carried by many graduates.

- Older, highly paid knowledge workers, professionals and middle managers may find that their jobs present plump targets for both offshoring and automation. Many of these people are likely to be middle aged with substantial family obligations, and will have few good prospects. Age discrimination lawsuits may well clog the courts of the future.

As I pointed out in Chapters 2 and 3, the long-term impact of a diminishing economic incentive for average people to pursue further education would be disastrous. In my opinion, this reality probably constitutes the single best argument for the adoption of an alternate income system that incorporates education as a primary incentive.

A rush for government jobs, and an increasing threat of taxpayer revolt

In the absence of competitive pressures, the government sector is far less susceptible to automation (and, of course, offshoring) than the private sector. As a result, government jobs may come to be perceived as safer, and the competition for these jobs may become intense. The United States may begin to look more like France, where nearly three quarters of students aspire to work for the government.[56]

In the wake of corporate layoffs, highly educated private sector workers, who have spent entire careers working 60 or more hour weeks, may find themselves with little to show for it—while at the same time, government clerks enjoy seemingly secure jobs, plush health care benefits and even defined benefit pension plans. The result is likely to be outrage, rejection of new taxes, and an ongoing conflict between private sector taxpayers and often unionized government workers.

Systemic unemployment invades the economy

At some point, evidence may be found that a new type of long-term unemployment is appearing—and increasing. It may initially be difficult to discern this new development from the lingering effects of the recession and from the traditionally high unemployment among certain groups. Nonetheless, it may eventually become apparent that this new, systemic unemployment cuts across a broad range of demographic groups. Specifically, we may see: even higher unemployment where we have come to expect it (unskilled workers, minorities, teenagers, etc.), unemployed recent college graduates, increasing numbers of older workers at every skill level who are unable to find work, retirees who cannot afford to stop working—but cannot find work, and a general problem with the "long-term unemployed." These will be people whose unemployment benefits have run out (perhaps multiple times). Political battles over the continuing extension of benefits may occur.

Eventually, this new systemic unemployment may begin to show up at nearly every educational and income level: from high school dropouts to former members of the "working wealthy." It's important to note that this unemployment will result from both the direct impact of automation and the indirect, economic impact associated with depressed consumer spending. Therefore, it will impact even people whose jobs are not in danger of being automated.

Increasingly bad news for entitlement and retirement programs

The current (already dire) forecasts for these programs most likely assume that younger workers will be fully employed. If systemic unemployment does appear, it will obviously undercut these assumptions. As I pointed out in Chapter 3, payroll taxes may become an unsustainable method of supporting these programs.

Trouble in China

If consumer spending in the U.S. and the rest of the developed world remains depressed, China may ultimately find it difficult to sustain the growth it needs to keep its workers employed. Giant retailers in the United States will likely continue to exert extreme pressure on Chinese manufacturers to produce ever cheaper, better and more sophisticated products. These businesses may have little choice but to turn increasingly to automation as a way to improve efficiency and trim costs. In a society that offers little in the way of a safety net, the saving rate among Chinese workers might remain very high, or perhaps even increase, in spite of the government's efforts to somehow spur consumer spending. All this may lead to increased incidents of civil unrest and instability.

Continuing Instability in the Financial Markets

As everyone knows, the current crisis began with the subprime meltdown. A case can certainly be made that stagnating wages played a role in the cause of that meltdown. Obviously, low wages made it difficult for these people to repay their loans.

Beyond that, I think it is also true that, to some degree, the motivation behind subprime loan programs was the idea of the "ownership society." Basically, in light of increasing evidence that wages paid to average people no longer offer a likely path to success, we turned instead to the promise of real estate speculation and tried to extend it to as many people as possible.

It didn't turn out well, and the lesson is that virtually all asset values in our economy are based on the assumption that we are going to continue having a vibrant mass market economy supported by robust consumer spending. If that basic assumption is threatened, we are very likely to see increased risk, volatility and, ultimately, deflating values. The "ownership society" idea just isn't workable—consumers need *incomes* (and confidence in the continuity of those incomes) to support the sustained discretionary spending that powers the economy. Remember: Everything that is produced by the economy is ultimately consumed by *individual human beings.*[1]

Ugly and irrational political battles

If trends similar to the ones I've listed above do develop, and if there is no coherent understanding and reasonable consensus regarding what is occurring, a dark scenario may develop. Political battles will become even more heated, partisan and irrational. Many politicians may act in even more purely self-interested ways as they come to genuinely fear the specter of their own unemployment.

Conservatives will likely cling to the idea that taxes should be cut on business even as it becomes clear that such cuts will result in little or no job creation. Liberals

---

[1] GDP is equal to Personal Consumer Spending + Business Investment (which occurs in anticipation of future consumer spending) + Net Exports (consumer spending in other countries) + Government Spending (money that the government spends to provide services to individual people). It all comes down to individual people buying stuff.

may call for increased job training even as the prospects for more educated workers are diminishing. They may also throw their weight behind organized labor, and this will lead to a continuing balkanization of the workforce into a protected elite versus a far larger number of highly vulnerable workers.

Outsmarting Marx

The central thesis of this book is that, as technology accelerates, machine automation may ultimately penetrate the economy to the extent that wages no longer provide the bulk of consumers with adequate discretionary income and confidence in the future. If this issue is not addressed, the result will be a downward economic spiral.

It must be acknowledged that this idea is quite similar to the predictions that were made by Karl Marx in the mid to late 1800s. Marx predicted that capitalism would suffer from a relentless "accumulation of capital," resulting in massive unemployment and wages that would be driven down below subsistence level. This in turn would result in diminished consumer demand, falling profits and ultimately economic crisis or even collapse.

If the arguments in this book prove correct, then we may be in the somewhat uncomfortable position of conceding that Marx was, at least in some ways, perceptive about the challenges the capitalist system would eventually encounter. That, of course, does not mean that we should consider adopting Marx's solution. He advocated the abolition of private property, a centrally planned economy, and perhaps most chillingly, the overthrow of governments and a "dictatorship of the proletariat." In the wake of the collapse of communism, these ideas have been shown unequivocally to be non-starters. They deserve to be swept into the dustbin of history.

The answer to the problem is clearly to adapt our system. The free market economy is not a natural phenomenon. It is really a machine that we have built and refined over centuries: it is an engine that is fundamentally driven by incentives. Marx wanted to take a sledgehammer to that engine. Our job is to tune it, and even re-engineer it if necessary, so that it will continue to power prosperity indefinitely.

The Technology Paradox

Most people who watch movies or have read science fiction novels are familiar with the potential paradoxes associated with time travel. For example, if you were able to travel back in time and then do something to prevent your parents from meeting before you were born, or perhaps kill a younger version of yourself, then you would presumably cease to exist. While we obviously don't need to worry too much about the practical problems of owning a time machine, I think that there is a somewhat analogous issue associated with the future of technology.

Many technologists who think deeply about the future believe that genuinely amazing things are possible. These visions include things such as truly intelligent machines and advanced nanotechnology that would allow us to transform matter, generate abundant clean energy and perhaps create tangible objects with the same ease that we now create graphics on a computer screen. There is also a great deal of speculation about fantastic medical advances that might cure major diseases and perhaps even dramatically extend the human lifespan. [1]

---

[1] While many diet books are a bit ambitious in terms of what they promise, Ray Kurzweil and Terry Grossman take things to an entirely new level with two books (*Fantastic Voyage: Live Long Enough to Live Forever* and *Transcend: Nine Steps to Living Well Forever*) based on the premise that if you can just hold on long enough to make it to the point of extraordinary technological acceleration (the "Singularity"), you should be able to take advantage of the continuous medical advances that will ensue, and then manage to become essentially immortal. You won't find many other books that discuss subjects such as

The essential point I want to make is that all this truly amazing stuff will require *enormous investment.* Certainly, trillions of dollars will need to be invested in order to make such technologies a reality. As I have pointed out throughout this book, such investment cannot occur in the absence of robust consumer demand. Within the context of the free market economy, no investor would make such an investment unless he or she anticipates a vibrant market for the resulting technology.

I would also argue that the level of automation I have been discussing in the book—in other words, the idea that a substantial fraction of routine, average jobs will be automated—represents a much lower point on the technology curve than all this really fantastic stuff. *Therefore, it will occur first.* As I have pointed out, if technology permanently eliminates huge numbers of workers—and creates pervasive fear in the minds of those who still have jobs—consumer demand would surely suffer dramatically. The bottom line is that, if our economic model is not adapted to the new reality, technology could essentially kill itself off. It is quite easy to imagine a scenario in which technology reached a certain point, but then slowed dramatically or even halted before getting to the really amazing things.

---

advanced artificial intelligence and cybernetics—and also have plenty of recipes for healthy dishes.

Machine Intelligence and the Turing Test

This book has primarily been concerned with the potential economic impact of what researchers in the field of artificial intelligence would call *narrow AI*. In other words, machines and software that are capable of sophisticated analysis, decision making and reasoning within a relatively narrow field of application. Such machines are not really intelligent in any meaningful sense—but they are highly competent at performing specific complex tasks and may well exceed the capability of a human worker.

Narrow AI applications are already in widespread use; expert systems such as the software that can autonomously pilot and land airliners and many of the advanced features built into Internet search engines and multiplayer role playing games fall into this area. Narrow AI is the practical side of artificial intelligence, and for that reason, we can expect that it will attract substantial commercial investment. As I have argued in this book, machines exhibiting vastly improved narrow AI capability may ultimately be poised to permanently take over a great many of the more routine jobs in the economy.

While narrow AI is increasingly deployed to solve real world problems and attracts most of the current commercial interest, the Holy Grail of artificial intelligence is, of course, *strong AI*—the construction of a truly intelligent machine. The realization of strong AI would mean the existence of a machine that is genuinely competitive with, or perhaps even superior to, a human being in its ability to reason and conceive ideas. The arguments I have made in this book do *not* depend on strong AI, but it is worth noting that if truly intelligent machines were built and became affordable, the trends I have predicted here would likely be amplified, and the economic impact would certainly be dramatic and might unfold in an accelerating fashion.

Research into strong AI has suffered because of some overly optimistic predictions and expectations back in the 1980s—long before computer hardware was fast enough to make true machine intelligence feasible. When reality fell far short of the projections, focus and financial backing shifted away from research into strong AI. Nonetheless, there is evidence that the vastly superior performance and affordability of today's processors is helping to revitalize the field.

Research into strong AI can be roughly divided into two main approaches. The direct computational approach attempts to extend traditional, algorithmic computing into the realm of true intelligence. This involves the development of sophisticated software applications that exhibit general reasoning. A second approach begins by attempting to understand and then simulate the human brain. The *Blue Brain Project*,[57] a collaboration between Switzerland's EPFL (one of Europe's top technical universities) and IBM, is one such effort to simulate the workings of the brain. Once researchers gain an understanding of the basic operating principles of the brain, it may be possible to build an artificial intelligence based on that framework. This would not be an exact replication of a human brain; instead, it would be something completely new, but based on a similar architecture.

When might strong AI become reality—if ever? I suspect that if you were to survey the top experts working in the field, you would get a fairly wide range of estimates. Optimists might say it will happen within the next 20 to 30 years. A more cautious group would place it 50 or more years in the future, and some might argue that it will never happen.

True machine intelligence is an idea that, in many ways, intrudes into the realm of philosophy, and for some people, perhaps even religion. What is the nature of intelligence? Is intelligence algorithmic? Can it be separated from consciousness or self-awareness? Roger Penrose, one of the world's top mathematical physicists, has written several books[58] suggesting that true artificial intelligence is unattainable using conventional computers because he believes that intelligence (or at least consciousness) has its roots in quantum mechanics—the area of physics that governs the probabilistic, and seemingly bizarre, interactions that occur between particles of subatomic size.

If strong AI does arrive, how will we know? That is a question that was first asked by Alan Turing nearly sixty years ago. Turing, a legendary British mathematician and code breaker during World War II, is often considered to be the founder of computer science. In 1950, Turing published a paper entitled "Computing Machinery and Intelligence," in which he proposed a test to answer the question: "Can machines think?"

Turing's test was based on a game popular at parties at the time. In today's terms, it amounts to a three-way instant messaging conversation. One participant is a human judge. The other participants are another person and a machine—both of whom attempt to convince the judge that they are human by conducting a normal conversation. If the judge can't tell which participant is which, then the machine is said to have passed the Turing Test.

The Turing Test is perhaps the most well-known and accepted method for measuring true machine intelligence. In practice, the rules would need to be further refined, and it seems likely that a panel of judges would be required rather than a single person. In my opinion, the main problem with the Turing Test is that it is, as Turing pointed out in his paper, an "imitation game." What it really tests is the ability of an intelligent entity to *imitate* a human being—it is not a test of intelligence itself. Presumably the conversation could roam into almost any area, so I think it is quite possible that an intelligent machine might be tripped up by a lack of actual human experience.

The realization of strong AI would mean that a true alien intelligence has appeared right here—rather than in the signals received from one of the radio telescopes used by the SETI project. We could not reasonably expect such an alien entity to think just like us or necessarily be able to replicate our experiences or outlook. My guess is that the best test for true machine intelligence will turn out to be similar to the standard devised by Supreme Court Justice Potter Stewart for obscenity: we'll know it when we see it.

If it does occur, the advent of genuinely intelligent machines will carry with it many potential perils for our society and economy.' However, there is a more subtle danger posed by the specter of strong AI: it distracts us from the far more immediate economic impacts that will likely result from narrow AI. Recent articles in the press[59] have pointed out that machines currently exhibit "insect-level" intelligence. In other words, if we were to set out to build a broadly intelligent machine today, we'd likely end up with something about as smart as a cockroach.

The problem with that comparison is that it gives us a false sense of security; it glosses over the obvious reality that cockroaches neither land aircraft nor defeat human beings at games of chess. When machine capability is focused narrowly, the story is very different. I think there is little doubt that in the coming years and decades, our definition of what constitutes "narrow" artificial intelligence is going to broaden quite dramatically. If it broadens to the degree that machines begin to encroach on a substantial fraction of the jobs that support consumers, the viability of capitalism will ultimately be threatened—unless, of course, our economic rules are adapted to reflect the new reality.

' These issues are beyond the scope of this book. For a good introduction to this area, I'd recommend reading "Why the future doesn't need us," an article written by Sun Microsystems co-founder Bill Joy for the April, 2000 issue of *Wired Magazine.*

Web: http://www.wired.com/wired/archive/8.04/joy.html

About / Contacting the Author

Martin Ford is the founder of a Silicon Valley-based software development firm. He has over 25 years experience in the fields of computer design and software development. He holds an MBA degree from the Anderson Graduate School of Management at UCLA and an undergraduate degree in computer engineering from the University of Michigan, Ann Arbor.

The author welcomes comments, criticisms and corrections and can be contacted by email at:

lightstunnel@yahoo.com.

The author also has a blog at:

http://econfuture.wordpress.com

NOTES

Introduction

[1] Larry Page on AI at Google: Web: http://news.cnet.com/2100-11395_3-6160372.html   video: http://news.cnet.com/1606-2_3-6160334.html?tag=mncol;txt

[2] Kurzweil has a $20,000 bet with Mitch Kapor that a computer will pass the "Turing Test" and thus exhibit human-like intelligence (see last section of the Appendix) by the year 2029. Web: http://www.longbets.org/1

Chapter 1: The Tunnel

[3] US Census Bureau, 2004, web: http://www.census.gov/Press-Release/www/releases/archives/education/004214.html

[4] Percentage of world's population in poverty, see the graph based on World Bank data at http://www.globalissues.org/article/26/poverty-facts-and-stats. My focus here is not on extreme poverty, which is measured at 1-3 dollars per day, but on an income level that prevents people from being viable mass market consumers.

[5] Doris Kearns Goodwin, *Team of Rivals: The Political Genius of Abraham Lincoln*, Simon and Schuster , 2005, p 77.

[6] "How deeply the curse of slavery...", Letter from William H. Seward to Albert H. Tracy, June 25, 1835. Albert H. Tracy Papers, New York State Library, Albany NY (as cited in *Team of Rivals*, p 77).

Chapter 2: Acceleration

[7] Punch cards at the University of Michigan: The university by then had a very advanced interactive time-sharing system called the "Michigan Terminal System" or MTS. Most students in advanced computer science and engineering courses used interactive terminals. However,

interactive computer time was very expensive, so punch cards were still used in introductory courses.

[8] Amdahl MIPS rating: Roy Longbottom's PC Benchmark Collection, Web: http://www.roylongbottom.org.uk/mips.htm#anchorAmdahl

[9] All computer MIPS ratings are taken from Wikipedia: http://en.wikipedia.org/wiki/Instructions_per_second. The MacIntosh and Lisa computers used the Motorola 68000 microprocessor with a rating of 1 MIPS.

[10] Calculating the amount in Bill's pocket: Google makes this easy. Just enter the following in the search box:

.01 * 2 ^ ((1986-1975)/2) (replace 1986 with the desired year)

[11] Ray Kurzweil, *The Singularity in Near: When Humans Transcend Biology*, New York, Penguin Group, 2005

[12] " "S" and "U" encoded within the interference patterns of quantum electron waves", Stanford News Service: http://news-service.stanford.edu/news/2009/january28/small-012809.html

[13] Many technologists believe that the exponential progress of information technology will ultimately level off. In other worlds, the graph will *someday* become an "s-curve," somewhat similar in shape to the graph of human capability that appears later in the "Diminishing Returns" section (see page 50). However, there is no way to know how far in the future this might occur, and there is little evidence to suggest it will happen anytime soon.

[14] For more on "quants" and the creation of exotic derivatives, see: Emmanuel Derman, *My Life as a Quant: Reflections on Physics and Finance*, New York, John Wiley and Sons, 2004.

[15] Charles Dickens, *Oliver Twist*.

[16] James J. Heckman and Paul A. LaFontaine, "The Declining American High School Graduation Rate: Evidence, Sources, And Consequences", *NBER Reporter*: Research Summary 2008, Number 1, web: http://www.nber.org/reporter/2008number1/heckman.html

[17] Literacy study, web:

http://nces.ed.gov/naal/estimates/overview.aspx

[18] SAT Scores, Wikipedia: http://en.wikipedia.org/wiki/SAT

[19] "Automation Takes Toll On Offshore Workers" by Paul McDougall, *InformationWeek*, January 26, 2004. Web:

http://www.informationweek.com/news/management/trends/show
Article.jhtml?articleID=17500858

[20] "The share of employment potentially affected by offshoring", Feb 23, 2006, Organisation for Economic Co-operation and Development (OECD). Web: http://www.oecd.org/dataoecd/37/26/36187829.pdf

[21] Table of Occupations taken from: Audrey Watson, "Employment and Wages of Typical U.S. Occupations", U.S. Bureau of Labor Statistics, May 2006. Web: http://www.bls.gov/oes/2006/may/typical.pdf

[22] "Tech's part in preventing attacks", Michael Kanellos, *CNET News*, July 7, 2005. Web: http://news.cnet.com/Techs-part-in-preventing-attacks/2100-7348_3-5778470.html

[23] Stack, Martin ; Gartland, Myles ; Keane, Timothy , "The offshoring of radiology: myths and realities", *SAM Advanced Management Journal*, January 1, 2007. Web:

http://www.accessmylibrary.com/coms2/summary_0286-
30757731_ITM

[24] "Nothing to lose but their chains," *The Economist*, June 19, 2008. Web:

http://www.economist.com/business/displayStory.cfm?source=hpte
xtfeature&story_id=11575170

[25] Jobs created by small business, see: SBA FAQ. Web:
http://www.sba.gov/advo/stats/sbfaq.pdf

[26] "Why so Nervous about robots, Wal-Mart?", July 8, 2005, Web:
http://news.cnet.com/8301-10784_3-5779674-7.html

[27] "Future Store" Web: http://www.future-store.org/fsi-
Internet/html/en/20412/index.html

[28] Ashlee Vance, "Microsoft Mapping Course to a Jetsons-style Future", *New York Times*, March 1, 2009, Web:
http://www.nytimes.com/2009/03/02/technology/business-computing/02compute.html?pagewanted=1&_r=4&hp

[29] P.W. Singer, *Wired for War: The Robotics Revolution and Conflict in the 21st Century*, New York, Penguin Press, 2009, pp 140-1.

[30] For more on nanotechnology and living organisms, see: Richard A. L. Jones, *Soft Machines: Nanotechnology and Life*, Oxford, Oxford University Press, 2004.

[31] Average wages by education level: U.S. Census Bureau News Release, January 10, 2008. Web: http://www.census.gov/Press-Release/www/releases/archives/education/011196.html

[32] William Easterly, *The Elusive Quest for Growth: Economists' Adventures and Misadventures in the Tropics*, Cambridge, MA, MIT Press, 2002, p.53.

[33] "Outsourcing not the Culprit in Manufacturing Job Loss", *AutomationWorld*, December 9th, 2003. Web:
http://www.automationworld.com/webonly-320

[34] Alan Greenspan, *The Age of Turbulence*, New York, The Penguin Press, 2007, p.397.

[35] *ABC News 20/20 Special*, "Last Days on Earth", 2006

[36] Kurzweil predicts the Technological Singularity by 2045: *Fortune Magazine*, May 14, 2007, Web:
http://money.cnn.com/magazines/fortune/fortune_archive/2007/05/14/100008848/

[37] "Vernor Vinge on the Singularity," Web:
http://mindstalk.net/vinge/vinge-sing.html

Chapter 3: Danger

[38] Robert J. Shapiro, *Futurecast: how superpowers, populations, and globalization will change the way you live and work*, New York, St. Martin's Press, 2008.

[39] Thomas L. Friedman, *The World is Flat: A Brief History of the Twenty First Century*, New York, Farrar, Strause and Giroux, 2005, 2006.

[40] China's high saving rate the result of government policy, see: Eamonn Fingleton, *In the Jaws of the Dragon: America's Fate in the Coming Era of Chinese Hegemony*, New York, St. Martin's Press, 2008.

[41] Pietra Rivoli, *The Travels of a T-Shirt in the Global Economy: An Economist Examines the Markets, Power and Politics of World Trade*, John Wiley and Sons, New York, 2005, p 40.

[42] Ibid. p 142.

[43] Jeff Rubin and Benjamin Tal, "Will Soaring Transport Costs Reverse Globalization?," *CIBC World Markets StrategEcon*, March 27, 2008. Web: http://yaleglobal.yale.edu/about/pdfs/oil.pdf

[44] Revenue per employee numbers. Source: Google Finance, based on 2008 revenue.

[45] "…growth without job creation." , *The Economist*, August 11, 2003. Web: http://www.economist.com/agenda/PrinterFriendly.cfm?Story_ID=1985889

[46] Huether, David, "The Case of the Missing Jobs, *BusinessWeek*, April 3, 2006. Web: http://www.businessweek.com/magazine/content/06_14/b3978116.htm

[47] Technically this might be better called "regressive" or "reverse progressive" since the deduction is higher at lower wage levels. However, those words have negative connotations…

[48] Fareed Zackaria, *The Future of Freedom: Illiberal Democracy at Home and Abroad*, New York, W.W. Norton & Co., 2003, p. 172-173.

[49] Blinder, Alan S., "Is Government too Political?" *Foreign Affairs*, November/December 1997. Web: http://www.foreignaffairs.org/19971101faessay3815/alan-s-blinder/is-government-too-political.html

[50] Jeremy Rifkin, *The End of Work: The Decline of the Global Labor Force and the Dawn of the Post-Market Era*, New York, Penguin Group, 1995.

Chapter 4: Transition

[51] Cornelia Dean, "Scientific Savvy? In U.S. Not Much", *New York Times*, August 30, 2005, web:

http://www.nytimes.com/2005/08/30/science/30profile.html

[52] See Chris Anderson's *The Long Tail: Why the Future of Business is Selling Less of More*, a book based on an article in *Wired Magazine*, October 2004. Web: http://www.wired.com/wired/archive/12.10/tail.html

[53] John Maynard Keynes, "Economic Possibilities for our Grandchildren," (written in 1930), *Essays in Persuasion*, New York, W.W. Norton, 1963. Web: http://www.econ.yale.edu/smith/econ116a/keynes1.pdf

p. 195 footnote, Einstein's view on technological unemployment, see: Walter Isaacson, *Einstein: His Life and Universe*, New York, Simon & Schuster, 2007, p.403.

Chapter 5: The Green Light

[54] For more on the challenges of addressing poverty, see: William Easterly, *The Elusive Quest for Growth: Economists' Adventures and Misadventures in the Tropics,* Cambridge, MA, MIT Press, 2002.

Appendix / Final Thoughts

[55] A.M Turing, "Computing Machinery and Intelligence", *Mind*, 1950. Web: http://loebner.net/Prizef/TuringArticle.html

[56] "French students shy of real world", *BBC News*, March 14, 2008. Web: http://news.bbc.co.uk/2/hi/europe/7293992.stm

[57] Blue Brain Project, Web: http://bluebrain.epfl.ch/

[58] Roger Penrose, The Emperor's New Mind: Concerning Computers, Minds, and the Laws of Physics, Oxford University Press, 1989 and

Shadows of the Mind: A Search for the Missing Science of Consciousness, Oxford University Press, 1994.

[59] For example: John Markoff, "Scientists worry that Machines may Outsmart Man", *New York Times*, July 25, 2009. Web: http://www.nytimes.com/2009/07/26/science/26robot.html?em

Made in the USA
San Bernardino, CA
03 July 2014